THE RIGHT TO KNOW AND THE RIGHT NOT TO KNOW

The Right to Know and the Right not to Know

Edited by
RUTH CHADWICK
MAIRI LEVITT
DARREN SHICKLE

Avebury

Aldershot · Brookfield USA · Hong Kong · Singapore · Sydney

Published by
Avebury
Ashgate Publishing Ltd
Gower House
Croft Road
Aldershot
Hants GU11 3HR
England

Ashgate Publishing Company
Old Post Road
Brookfield
Vermont 05036
USA

British Library Cataloguing in Publication Data

The right to know and the right not to know. - (Avebury
        series in philosophy)
        1. Human chromosome abnormalities - Diagnosis - Moral and
        ethical aspects 2. Disease susceptibility - Genetic aspects
        - Moral and ethical aspects 3. Genetic disorders - Moral and
        ethical aspects
        I. Chadwick, Ruth F. II. Levitt, Mairi III. Shickle, Darren
        174.2'5

        ISBN 1 85972 424 8

Library of Congress Catalog Card Number: 96-79376

Printed in Great Britain by
Antony Rowe Ltd, Chippenham, Wiltshire

Contents

Figures and tables

Acknowledgements

The contributors are grateful to the Commission of the European Communities for funding the Euroscreen 1 project (1994 - 1996) which investigated the ethical and philosophical issues raised by developments in genetic screening. This book forms part of the Euroscreen 1 project. Thanks are also due to Kerry Wilding, the Euroscreen Administrator, for her invaluable help in preparing the manuscript for publication.

List of contributors

Ruth Chadwick is Head of Centre and Professor of Moral Philosophy in the Centre for Professional Ethics at the University of Central Lancashire. She is co-ordinator of two multidisciplinary and multinational research projects funded by the European Union; Euroscreen - genetic screening: ethical and philosophical perspectives, and Biocult: cultural and social objections to biotechnology - an analysis of the arguments, with special reference to the views of young people. Her publications include the four volume edited collection, *Kant: Critical Assessments; Ethics, Reproduction and Genetic Control;* and a large number of papers in learned journals. She is joint series editor of the Routledge series on Professional Ethics. She is Secretary of the International Association of Bioethics and a member of the National Committee for Philosophy.

Urban Wiesing is lecturer at the Institute for Theory and History of Medicine at the University of Münster and visiting lecturer for medical ethics at the University of Tübingen. His publications *include Die In-vitro-Fertilisation - ein umstrittenes Experiment* (Springer, 1991, together with Christina Hölze), *Kunst oder Wissenschaft? Konzeption der Medizin in der deutschen Romantik* (Frommann-Holzboog, 1995), *Zur Verantwortung des Arztes* (Frommann-Holzboog, 1995). Together with Richard Toellner he edited *Wissen - Handeln - Ethiek. Strukturen ärztlichen Hendelns und ihre ethische Relevanz* (Gustav Fischer Verlag, 1995).

Mairi Levitt is a sociologist working in the Centre for Professional Ethics. She is a member of the core group of Euroscreen and was prinicipal investigator on the Biocult project. Her research interests are in attitudes and values in relation to health, education and religion. She has recently published *Nice when they are young: Contemporary Christianity in families and schools* (Avebury, 1996).

Ingmar Pörn is Professor of Philosophy at the University of Helsinki. His publications include *The Logic of Power*, *Element of Social Analysis* and *Action Theory and Social Science*. In recent years he has published papers on health and disease, emotions and the meaning of life. He is currently working on the conceptual foundations of care and caring.

Tony McGleenan is lecturer in Jurisprudence at the Queen's University of Belfast, a member of the core goup of the Euroscreen project and currently coordinates a research group which assesses the impact of genetic screening on the insurance industry. He has published journal articles in the field of medical law and ethics and a number of essays on legal responses to genetic technology.

Jørgen Husted is associate Professor of Philosophy, University of Aarhus. He is a member of the Danish Council of Ethics and Senior Research Fellow in the Danish Research Council Programme: 'Bioethics - foundations and applications'. He has published in the areas: philosophy of language, epistemology, general ethics and bioethics.

Darren Shickle is a lecturer at the Centre for Applied Public Health Medicine, University of Wales College of Medicine. He is currently a 1996/97 Harkness Fellow visiting the Bioethics Institute, John Hopkins University, Baltimore and the Kennedy Institute of Bioethics, Georgetown University, Washington D.C., U.S.A. His research interests are Public Health Ethics and Medical Genetics.

Henk ten Have is Professor of Medical Ethics at the School of Medical Sciences, Katholieke Universiteit, Nijmegen, the Netherlands. He is also Visiting Professor at the Centre for Professional Ethics, University of Central Lancashire. His publications include *Geneeskunde tussen droom en drama* (Kok Agora, 1986), *The Growth of Medical Knowledge* (Kluwer, 1990, edited with G. Kisma and S. Spicker). He is chief editor of Ethiek en Recht in de Gezondheidszorg (Kluwer, 1990 - 1996). He is co-founder and secretary of the European Society for Philosophy of Medicine and Health Care.

Introduction

According to Aristotle 'all men by nature are actuated with the desire of knowledge' (1991). As evidence for this Aristotle proposes the love of the senses especially that of sight, 'for even, irrespective of their utility, are they loved for their own sakes'. However do all men and women desire to know, or more specifically in the context of this book, is there a desire to know about genetic status, whether it be their own or that of someone else?

While the individual has an obvious interest in knowing about their genetic status, there will be others who may be interested in knowing, for differing reasons and with differing degrees of legitimacy:

1　blood relatives (i.e. others with the gene or are at risk of the gene)
2　other family members (e.g. spouse, who are potential carers)
3　friends (who may be altruistically interested in the patient's well-being)
4　health care system or the insurance company who may pay for the test or subsequent health care
5　employers who have made investments in training or who may have responsibility under health and safety regulations for their employees.

Right to know versus right not to know

Certainly an overwhelming majority of the public think that genetic screening is a good idea and when asked, hypothetically, whether they would want to be tested themselves, most say that they would. For example, prior to establishing mass carrier screening for cystic fibrosis, a number of surveys were performed to establish the level of public interest in being tested. The research suggested that

1

demand would be high. However, when a real offer of screening is made as part of a screening programme, the uptake is considerably lower.

Even among families at high risk for a genetic disorder, many individuals choose not to know. For example, Tyler et al. reviewed the experience of genetic centres in the UK with pre-symptomatic testing for Huntington's disease between 1987 and 1990 (testing in the UK was first performed in 1987). They commented that demand for testing was 'much less than expected as surveys carried out before linkage was possible suggested that between 56 percent and 66 percent of people at risk would make use of a predictive test if it were available'. In practice only 248 tests were performed in the first years of test availability, which is a very small proportion of the estimated 10,000 people at a 50 percent risk of the disease (Tyler, Ball and Craufaud, 1992, p. 1594)

Right to hope versus right to certainty

The low uptake of Huntington's disease predictive testing is a challenge to Aristotle's assertion on the desire to know. Colloquially, in addition to 'knowledge is power' the saying 'ignorance is bliss' is also used. This apparent contradiction recognises that individuals will differ in their attitude to risk. Some individuals may have a positive preference for taking risks i.e. are 'risk lovers'. Others will prefer to minimise risk taking i.e. are 'risk adverse'. Other individuals will be risk neutral (O'Brien, 1986).

The way in which a person responds to an offer of screening will depend on a number of factors. The Health Belief Model suggests that the likelihood of taking a health action depends on the perceived threat of disease and perceived benefits and barriers. The perceived threat of disease is dependent on the perceptions of susceptibility to the disease and of its severity.

An asymptomatic young person with a parent affected by Huntington's disease has a 50 percent risk of developing the disease themselves. Such a person may prefer to have uncertainty about their fate removed. If the test is negative the 'death threat' is removed. Patients with negative results could be spared the intensive monitoring that members of families at high risk of genetic disorders such as familial polyposis coli tend to be offered. Even if the result of the predictive test is positive, these individuals can make preparations for the time when they begin to become symptomatic.

For some genetic disorders there may be preventive measures that could be taken. For example a woman who has inherited the BRCA1 gene is likely to develop breast cancer. Some such women choose to undergo prophylactic bilateral mastectomy. Alternatively, regular follow-up could be offered to identify breast cancer at an early stage.

Carriers of abnormal genes for autosomal disorders can modify their reproductive choices once they are made aware of their risk status. These may include deciding not to have children, adoption, artificial insemination by donor, or attempting a pregnancy with prenatal diagnosis.

In contrast, the 'risk lovers' may wish to retain the hope that they have not inherited the gene. Some people may not be able to cope with the 'label' associated with a positive genetic test result. The psychological distress may significantly affect quality of life. Even patients with negative test results can suffer as a consequence. Some people experience guilt at their 'good fortune' if a sibling is found to be affected.

Can you decide not to know without knowing what there is to know?

Most of the cohort of people at risk of Huntington's disease will have been aware of their risk status; the nature of autosomal dominant diseases means that an 'at risk' individual will usually have an affected parent (some mutations will be spontaneous, while some cases will may not have diagnosed correctly). These families will usually be acutely aware of the nature of the disease and its inheritance. However, for many other genetic disorders e.g. cystic fibrosis, there will be no recent family history of the disease.

There is an apparent incongruity in the 'right to know, right not to know' debate. How can an ignorant person remain ignorant once they have been asked whether they want to know whether they have, or are at risk of having a particular gene? The very fact that they are being asked suggests that they are at a level of risk that justifies the asking of the question. It would not therefore be possible to say 'no thank you, I do not want to know that I am at risk', because their ignorance has been destroyed. It would only be possible to refuse the offer of further information that would modify their a priori risk. The loss of ignorance is irreversible and hence genetic counselling may be more analogous to a surgical procedure than drug therapy.

A duty to know as much as possible?

There seems to be consensus within the philosophical literature that the acquisition of knowledge is good. Ethical problems tend to arise if the knowledge is abused. If 'knowledge is a good thing' is it also true that 'the more knowledge the better'? Further is there a duty to gain as much knowledge as possible?

An international survey of geneticists reported that virtually all respondents believed that an absolutely essential goal of genetic screening was to 'help patients understand their options so they can make decisions' (Wertz and Fletcher, 1988). Can a fully autonomous individual make an informed choice with only partial knowledge i.e. an asymptomatic person at risk of Huntington's disease may be aware that they are at 50 percent risk of carrying the gene and make reproductive choices accordingly. The predictive test would usually be able to change this risk to 0 percent or 100 percent. Is it necessary for them to be tested in order to make a truly informed choice?

Most decisions are made without complete information. Consent to surgery is normally considered to be informed if the doctor has adequately explained what the procedure involves, the potential benefits of the operation and the common and/or important complications. However, it is not necessary for the patient to have studied at medical school or even to have trained for many additional years in the surgical speciality in order to obtain all possible information. Similarly, I may choose to catch a train, knowing that it will be at the station at just after 11 o'clock; it is not necessary to know that it leaves at 11.03 in order to decide when I should leave the house. Thus, it may not be necessary to know a more accurate genetic risk in order to make reproductive or other life choices.

A right to confidentiality?

Within medical practice there is an expectation that confidentiality will be maintained. For example, the Hippocratic Oath contains the phrase:

> Whatever, in connection with my professional practice, or not in connection with it, I see or hear, in the life of men, which ought not to be spoken of abroad, I will not divulge, as reckoning that all such should be kept secret (BMA, 1993, p. 326).

Within professional codes of conduct it is usually stipulated that patients are entitled to expect that the information that a doctor learns during the course of a medical consultation, investigation or treatment will remain confidential. Doctors therefore have a duty not to disclose to any third party except when disclosure is required by statute, in the public interest, or in connection with judicial proceedings.

However, the General Medical Council has recognised that:

> Special problems relating to confidentiality can arise where doctors have responsibilities not only to patients but also to third parties as, for example, where a doctor assesses a patient for an employer or an insurance company (General Medical Council, 1992, para. 90).

4

A duty to let others know?

A report of the Royal College of Physicians of the UK (1991) quoted two cases where an individual may wish to exercise a right to prevent others from knowing. However, public interest may mean that there is a duty to let others know.

> A lorry-driver from a family who could reasonably be considered to have Huntington's chorea from which his father appeared to have died, was involved in a major accident. A year or two later, he was involved in a frontal collision with another driver, and continued the conflict in hand-to-hand fighting with the other driver until separated by the police, after which his licence was removed. When seen by a geneticist, he was showing signs of Huntington's chorea, and was unemployed and seriously depressed. A consultant neurologist had written in his behalf, stating that if his licence were returned his depression would improve. What should the geneticist do?

> A surgeon consulted a clinical geneticist concerning myotonic dystrophy, from which he and his father suffered. The diagnosis was not in doubt. His cataracts had been removed, and he had difficulty in letting go of his instruments. Should the geneticist inform this man's employers?

In both these cases the Report is questioning whether the geneticist is under a duty of disclosure. However, there may also be a responsibility on the patient to let others know. Rights are balanced by responsibilities.

A duty to let family know?

A particular category of interested third parties are other family members who either may have an obligation to care for their 'loved ones' with a genetic disease, or may themselves be at risk of carrying an abnormal gene or of developing the genetic disorder themselves. This conflict of interests has been recognised by a number reports of genetics. For example the Committee on the Ethics of Gene Therapy (Clothier Report, 1992, para. 4.15) recognised that the duty of confidentiality is balanced by a duty of disclosure:

> An individual might be the source of genetic information which is important to relatives. It might be important to their health care, decisions on parenthood, or life plans which might be influenced by known health risks ... These factors have a bearing on the confidentiality of such information and the circumstances in which it might be disclosed.

The Royal College of Physicians of the UK also suggested that:

> Because of the nature of genes, it may be argued that genetic information about any individual should not be regarded as personal to that individual, but as the common property of other people who may share those genes, and who need the information in order to find out their own genetic constitution (1991, para. 4.10)

The Nuffield Council Report suggested that:

> there would be a stronger case for overriding individuals' objections where the information would influence a decision having potentially damaging rather than merely inconvenient consequences for other family members (Nuffield Council on Bioethics, 1993).

The British Medical Association have stated that:

> Certainty about an individual's genotype might affect his attitudes to life, and society's attitudes to him, with the possibility of considerable medical, economic and social repercussions. The importance of such information probably outweighs the importance of complete individual medical confidentiality ... (BMA, 1980, p. 30)

A right to ignorance?

Autonomous individuals may decide to reject a genetic test because they do not wish to know their genetic status. However, the nature of genetic inheritance means that an individual's genetic status will become apparent through the testing of a relative. Just as a parent will discover that they carry a cystic fibrosis gene if one of their children is diagnosed as having cystic fibrosis, a genetic test will also reveal information about other family members and their risk of having a particular gene.

There will therefore be a tension between the right of, for example, one identical twin to know and for the other not to know. Similarly, if a person with a grandparent who died of Huntington's disease undergoes predictive testing and is also found to have the disease, then the gene must be present in the intervening generation. It may be possible not to disclose the result of these tests to the family member who did not want to be tested themselves, but the nature of family interaction means that it is very difficult to maintain this secrecy.

John Stuart Mill in his essay *On Liberty* recognised that the right of an individual to make autonomous choices is associated with a duty not to infringe the rights of others to exercise their autonomy. Thus he argued that freedom means:

doing as we like, subject to such consequences as may follow: without impediment from our fellow creatures so long as what we do does not harm them ... nor attempt to deprive others of theirs, or impede their efforts to obtain it (Mill, 1975, p. 18)

The tension between the autonomous desires of two parties, especially if they are family members, is best resolved by the individuals themselves. Whilst a geneticist should respect the wishes of their patient to be tested or not, they should encourage their client to consider the implications and implications for others who will be affected.

Autonomy versus solidarity

There is an increasing respect for the autonomy of the individual over community values, especially in North America and Western Europe. However, in practice such conflicts of interest are rare. In a report from The Netherlands, solidarity has been defined as:

> an awareness of unity and a willingness to bear the consequences of it. Unity indicates the presence of a group of people - for example, family, religious group, ethnic subpopulation - with a common history and common convictions and ideals (Government Committee on Choices in Health Care, 1992, p. 56).

One of the features of solidarity is that it is reciprocal. As part of group solidarity, an individual would act in the interests of a fellow group member, even though this action may not be their preferred option. Thus a genetic counsellor may say to a client: 'if your sister were in your position, would you want her to disclose the information'?

A right to know versus a right not to know about genetic status: new ethical problems?

Most of the various tensions identified between rights to know and not to know are not specific to genetics.

Uptake rates of less than 100 percent are to be expected from any form of screening programme. In these other types of screening programmes many 'non-responders' will be making conscious decisions that they do not want to know.

The rights of patients to confidentiality and public interest exemptions are discussed in professional codes of ethics. In the UK, for example, when a patient is diagnosed as having epilepsy, a doctor is obliged to contact the Driver Vehicle

Licensing Authority. The driving licence is suspended until the patient has not had a fit for two years. Similarly employers have an interest in knowing whether an employee has a non-genetic illness that affects their ability to perform their job, or is a danger to other employees under health and safety regulations.

Patients diagnosed as being HIV positive may wish to limit those who know about their status. If they wish to withold this information from a sexual partner there are analogies with one of the genetic examples. The partner if told may wish to be tested and may also have a right to know in order to take precautions against becoming infected. Sexual partners would want to ensure that any sexual contact is 'safe'. However, it could be argued that other friends and family may need to know in order that they handle spillage of bodily fluids appropriately. Of course it could be argued that all sex should be safe or that any body fluid spillage should be treated with care, irrespective of HIV status.

The right to know and the right not to know

The papers contained in this book deal with some of these conflicts of rights in more detail from different perspectives: philosophy, history of medicine, sociology, law and public health.

The first four papers were presented by members of the Euroscreen project on genetic screening: ethical and philosophical perspectives (see Appendix I) at an international symposium on gene ethics at the University of Turku, Finland in August 1995. Ruth Chadwick identifies the central concepts in the debate as autonomy, confidentiality, privacy and solidarity and considers these concepts in her discussion of the questions 'whose right?' and 'to know what?' Individuals may claim a right to know about their own or another's genetic consitution, as may institutions, but the so-called knowledge deals with probabilities. Chadwick discusses whether there are justifications for overriding the rights of confidentiality and autonomy in the area of genetics. Arguments for a right *not* to know may be based on considerations of privacy, integrity and self-determination, but there are counter-arguments emphasising solidarity and responsibility. She concludes that the different types of genetic information and conditions prevent asimple assertion of a right either to know or not to know.

Urban Wiesing's chapter provides a comment on the same issue from an historical perspective and asks whether stories about the past justifiably influence moral decisions. Having considered the role of historical evidence in ethics he focuses on genetics during the Nazi era in Germany and the guidance that the history of genetics can offer to the present day, arguing for substantial protection of individual rights against any purported rights of society. In the third chapter Mairi Levitt puts the debate in social context by taking a sociological perspective. She discusses the theme of individual responsibility for health found in health campaigns and advertising and the interests such individualisation might serve. A consideration of different types of genetic information points to benefits and disbenefits. While those who already know they, or their children, are at risk may welcome genetic information, the health of the less privileged would in general be better served by a reduction of social inequalities than by an extension of routine genetic screening.

Ingmar Pörn's paper demonstrates the importance of examining the type of particular rights claims that might be made in the right to know/not to know debate, because the correct specification of a rights claim by person X has implications for what would be required of other people e.g. whether they have a duty to take any action to bring it about that X's right may be exercised. In elucidating the meaning of rights in the debate Pörn draws on Hohfeld's analysis of rights to argue for an interpretation in terms of freedom of choice for the individual, implying a prohibition on the professional from interfering. Interestingly, however, Pörn suggests that there might be exceptions to this position.

Tony McGleenan examines the possibility of a legal framework for rights to know and not to know; in particular whether there is a need for a genetic privacy law. Despite the primacy of the concept in the legal system of the United States, the ethical basis of privacy is not well developed. Privacy conflicts with other interests such as solidarity, which is of particular importance in the context of genetic information. McGleenan goes on to discuss the ELSI Genetic Privacy Act and argues that legislators would do better to target the misuse of genetic information rather than introduce laws to protect privacy itself. The latter may undermine a sense of social solidarity which is arguably an important form of protection against threats such as genetic determinism.

Jørgen Husted focuses on the specific issue of unsolicited disclosure of genetic information to hitherto unsuspecting relatives, who thereby irreversibly lose their 'genetic inncocence' and thus their right not to know. In thinking about the moral acceptability of this - about whether it can be justified in terms of a right to know - it is important to distinguish between two sense of autonomy: a thin and a thick conception. From the point of view of the thin conception the disclosure appears to enhance autonomy by providing information to facilitate decision-making. This analysis is flawed if a thick conception allowing for autonomy as self-*definition* is acknowledged, however, because it takes the decision of whether to know or not to know itself away from the individual. There are dangers here of moralism as well as paternalism.

Darren Shickle widens the debate about the right to know and not to know from the individual to the population. He argues that there may be a right of society not to know certain things, such as the genetic basis of intelligence, because of the undesirable social consequences that may ensue. Against the claim of scientists of a right to know, by being free to engage in research, he suggests that scientists have a duty to use their skills responsibly and he discusses the possibility of a moratorium in certain areas.

The role of the media in raising public awareness of advances in genetics, in particular genetic screening, is considered in the paper by Ruth Chadwick and

Mairi Levitt which is based on a survey of the quality press in the UK. For each new development in genetic screening it was found that media reports began with uncritical reporting based on medical sources. Once screening programmes were under way reports would typically incorporate patient experience and medical evidence. When the technique is actually used and real individuals are involved then the ethical dilemmas brought by greater knowledge become apparent. Journalists did not distort or oversimplify the issues, rather their stories followed the progression from the wonder of new scientific discoveries and their possibilities to the practical dilemmas when the knowledge is put to everyday use.

In the final article Henk ten Have acknowledges the importance of media representations as part of the cultural context in which genetic discoveries are promulgated. Discussion of the right to know and not to know needs to take this into account and not simply concentrate on the individual. We live with the possibility of a 'geneticized' future, partly because of the tendency to link knowledge and its application and partly because of a prevailing consensus about two ideals: non-directiveness in counselling and individual responsibility for health, both of which encourage the idea that it is good to know as much as possible. What is required is prior discussion over the goals at which we should aim; the uses to which genetic knowledge should be put. In this debate there are two factors, in particular, which may counteract the trend towards geneticization: the need to distinguish between disease and health, and the fact that there are norms inherent in medicine which diverge from non-directiveness.

As genetic screening and testing increase in scope and accuracy, the ability of human beings to reflect on their genetic inheritance ensures that the right to know and the right not to know will continue to be debated.

References

Aristotle (1991), *The Metaphysics*, trans. McMahon, J.H, Buffalo: Prometheus Books.
British Medical Association, (1980), *The Handbook of Medical Ethics*, p. 30, British Medical Association: London.
British Medical Association, (1993*), Medical Ethics Today: Its Practice and Philosophy*, p. 326, British Medical Association: London
Clothier Report (1992), *Report of the Committee on the Ethics of Gene Therapy* (Clothier Report), Cm.1788, para. 4.15, HMSO: London.
General Medical Council, (1992*), Professional Conduct and Discipline: Fitness to Practise*, para. 90, General Medical Council: London.
Govenment Committee on Choices in Health Care, The Netherlands (1992), *Choices in Health Care*, Ministry of Welfare, Health and Cultural Affairs, Rijswijk: The Netherlands.
Mill, J.S. (1975), *Three Essays: On Liberty, Representative Government and The Subjection of Women*, Oxford University Press: Oxford.

Nuffield Council on Bioethics (1993), *Genetic Screening Ethical Issues*, Nuffield Council on Bioethics: London.

O'Brien B. (1986), *'What are My Chances Doctor?- A Review of Clinical Risks'*, Office of Health Economics: London.

Royal College of Physicians Committees on Ethical Issues in Medicine and Clinical Genetics (1991), *Ethical Issues in Clinical Genetics*, para. 4.10, Royal College of Physicians: London.

Tyler, A., Ball, D. and Craufaud, D. (1992), 'Presymptomatic testing for Huntington's disease in the United Kingdom', *British Medical Journal*, Vol.304, pp.1593-1596.

Wertz, D.C. and Fletcher, J.C. (1988), 'Attitudes of Genetic Counsellors: a Multinational Survey', *American Journal of Genetics*, Vol. 42, pp. 592-600.

1   The philosophy of the right to know and the right not to know

Ruth Chadwick

To know what?

When discussion in the context of clinical genetics turns to the right to know, the right not to know is increasingly asserted, so consideration of the one inevitably requires consideration of the other. But before we can examine the basis of these purported rights, a number of preliminary clarifications are in order. First, in talking of rights to know or not to know I am not assuming any particular view about the existence of rights. What I am concerned with are the reasons that might be given in support of the claim of a right to know or not to know, which might have different theoretical bases. Second, questions arise concerning whose right? *and* to know what?

There are at least four central concepts in the right to know/right not to know debate: autonomy, confidentiality, privacy and solidarity. Regarding the first of the two questions identified above, 'Whose right?' there is an interesting difference between the right to know and the right not to know. The right not to know is typically claimed by a person who does not want to have access to information about themselves, perhaps in a response to claims by others to have that information. And this point suggests why the right *to* know may be claimed not only by the individual concerned but also by a variety of third parties who want access to information about someone else. Hence confidentiality has provided a focus for much of the discussion of the right to know - in other words, the circumstances in which a third party's interest in some knowledge becomes sufficiently great to justify disclosure; in the case of the right not to know, however, we find privacy playing a larger part. But of course there are other concepts and arguments in both cases.

The right to know what? Presumably information about an individual's genetic constitution. Here, however, there is a variety of possibilities. What might be at stake is knowledge that an individual carries a recessive gene such as sickle cell; or a dominant one such as the Huntington's gene. Or it might be a predisposition to a multifactorial condition such as coronary heart disease or breast cancer. But an important distinction has to be made between genetic determination and genetic predisposition. Genetic information about a person, it has been claimed (Harper, 1992) is different from other medical information about a person because it has the following features, among others: it is independent of age, it is independent of clinical state (which may be mild or severe, now or never); it is independent of tissue. To know that someone has a genetic predisposition does not tell us when or in many cases if or to what extent he or she will develop the condition in question. This point has special relevance in the case of predispositions to multifactorial conditions.

Genetic so-called 'knowledge', then, deals with probabilities. In particular cases the predictive power of genetic tests may be a factor in assessing the strength of claims of third parties to have access to genetic information, depending on the theoretical justification to which appeal is made. This particular issue, however, I mention only to set aside for present purposes.

The right to know

The right to know one's own genetic constitution

This claim I do not propose to discuss in great detail, because it is the least different from other areas of medicine and raises similar issues to claims of right to knowledge about one's medical condition, based on principles of autonomy and self-determination. The knowledge may enable the individual to seek appropriate therapy or to take preventive or ameliorative action. There is however an added dimension to the right in the context of genetics which is brought out by the Royal College of Physicians of London (1991, para. 4.7) point that individuals have the right to make reproductive decisions in the light of as much information as possible. Whereas access to information will always be important in making plans and life choices, genetic information is relevant to *reproductive* choice.

The right to know the genetic constitution of another

Does anyone else have a right to genetic information about another? Is there not a presumption that medical information is confidential? The majority of statements about confidentiality allow for some limited exceptions (see the fuller discussion in Ngwena and Chadwick, 1993). Much depends on what the grounds are for supporting confidentiality. If it is supported on the basis of autonomy (interpreted in terms of allowing the individual control over who has access to him or herself), then allowance has to be made for the fact that respecting the

14

autonomy and confidentiality of one person may have implications for the autonomy of others in so far as it affects *their* capacity to make autonomous reproductive decisions.

In deciding between the autonomy of different parties, the decision cannot be taken *on autonomy grounds* alone. It is arguable that in the context of the client/professional relationship, the burden of proof has to be on the one who would break a confidence because of the special nature of that relationship. But on what grounds could a justification be given?

If utility is the ground for confidentiality then it might be justifiable to break confidentiality when protecting it will *not* maximise expected utility - for example, in a case where non-disclosure leads to the avoidable birth of a handicapped child. Confidentiality, on this approach, might appear to be quite vulnerable, but it is not as vulnerable as it might seem if the side effects on society as a whole are taken into consideration. The wider implications for trust in the client/professional relationship generally have to be considered. Also, the utility calculation is not always easy. Consider a case, of a type not infrequently discussed, where a woman in her forties has been found to carry the Huntington's gene. Let us suppose that she has a grown up daughter who is planning to stop using contraception and start a family. The mother, however, does not want her daughter to know about her genetic status, even though it is clearly relevant to her daughter's plans. Both have the same doctor. It might be argued that here the greater utility would be gained by the doctor breaking a confidence: that the mother's utility gain can surely not outweigh the potential utility loss to the daughter. But what exactly might the daughter's utility loss be? She may carry the gene herself or she may not. If she does, she may subsequently come to resent the fact that she was deceived. She may give birth to a child who also has the gene, an outcome which, given her preferences, she would not have chosen had she known. In the latter scenario however not only would she have forfeited parenthood, but also the child would have been denied the possibility of say 40 years of disease-free life. The potential disutility is also in the future, and only possible, whereas the mother's desire to keep a secret is here and now. (The reason why she wants to keep a secret is not obvious, but may be connected with fear that attitudes towards her may change or with the aim of protecting her daughter from unpleasant news now). The matter is not clear on utility grounds, but it is an approach that can not only offer reasons why confidentiality is important, but also take into account the circumstances in which other interests might take priority.

It is important to note that on this position, it is assumed that a breach of confidentiality requires a justification. In general there are strong enough reasons of a utilitarian kind to underpin a presumption in favour of confidentiality. This presumption, however, has arguably been weakened in the context of genetics. The Royal College of Physicians Report on *Ethical Issues in Clinical Genetics* for example, suggests 'reasons for considering whether, in certain limited cases, the usually accepted rights of patients and others to autonomy and confidentiality should be reconsidered. These cases concern (a) the special concern of genetics with decisions about having children, and (b) problems with what might be called the ownership of genes' (Royal College of Physicians, 1991, para. 2.5).

Putting aside the ownership issue, which is beyond the scope of this discussion, there is at least a suggestion here that there are competing considerations in the sphere of reproduction which have to be considered, alongside the individual's claim to confidentiality.

It might be argued that the spouse or partner has a right to informed reproductive decision-making, e.g. on autonomy grounds. If it is held that individuals have the right to make reproductive decisions in the light of as much information as possible, then to deny a person information that might be pertinent to his or her decision is a harm, in so far as it violates a right. It is not clear, however, why, even if it is accepted that this is a right, choice in this area should be given a higher priority than choice in the use of personal information.

From a different, consequentialist, point of view a harm that might be considered relevant, however, is the cost (financial, emotional and physical) of rearing a handicapped child. It may involve, for example, forgoing employment to provide care. Someone who is aware of relevant genetic information can take steps to avoid these costs.

There are arguments to suggest that not only is there a *right* to make reproductive decisions on the basis of as much information but also a *duty* to do so (Royal College of Physicians, 1991, para. 4.7). Kielstein and Sass, for example, speak of a 'duty to know' which is based on the principle of *responsible parenthood* (Kielstein and Sass, 1992, p. 401). The grounds on which such a duty might be based could include the welfare of as yet unborn generations and/or the need to reduce costs to society.

The above discussion has been based on the assumption that the issue concerns the possible grounds for overriding the interest of an autonomous adult in confidentiality. There are analogous arguments, however, about neonatal screening, to the effect that parents have a right to genetic information about an existing child to facilitate their future reproductive choice (Laird et al., 1996).

The right of institutions to know

In addition to the claimed rights of other individuals to access to genetic information, there are arguments for the rights of institutions such as insurance companies. They have an interest in genetic information about individuals, with the possible options of charging a higher premium or restricting cover. Much depends here on how such institutions are to be regarded from a philosophical point of view, for example whether insurance companies are simply businesses with the aim of maximising profit or whether they also serve a social purpose. If the former, then from a liberal perspective it is a matter of balancing their interests in access to information with the interests of the individual in confidentiality. These are in competition, because the individual has a chance of having genetic testing and then securing favourable terms by keeping this information quiet. From a communitarian perspective the industry serves a social purpose in spreading risks in society, and individuals also have responsibilities to other members of society (e.g. not to drive up premiums for everybody by dishonesty). A further problem is the suggestion that genetics has the potential to undermine the whole conceptual basis of insurance by its capacity to differentiate the population in a very precise way (Chadwick and Ngwena, 1995) .

Arguments for a right not to know

As stated above, the argument for a right not to know is typically made by or on behalf of an individual e.g. when a third party wants access to information, which he or she does not wish to know about himself or herself - when a genetic relative wants it, or an insurer wants it, or an employer requires pre-employment screening. It is important to recognise however that it is not simply a case of X wanting information about Y. X may want information about X which will inevitably give Y information about Y which Y does not want. Suppose, for example, that of two genetically identical twins, one wants to be tested for a genetic predisposition and the other does not. Even if the one who is tested agrees not to disclose to the other the result of a test, the choices he or she makes thereafter may be revealing.

What are the arguments for a right not to know?

The negative approach

One strategy that might be adopted is the negative one of making the case that the arguments for a right *to* know are inadequate. Stone and Stewart (1996) have argued that there is insufficient evidence to support the claims of screening enthusiasts. They ask 'Armed with genetic knowledge, do people actually use it in reproductive decision-making or in long-term planning?' and argue that 'The danger is that a combination of technical capability, professional zeal and consumer demand will lead to a 'right to know' imperative which will override currently accepted screening principles' (Stone and Stewart, 1996, pp. 4-5). As far as the moral argument is concerned, however, whether or not people do actually use the information in particular ways cannot by itself determine whether or not they have the right to it. It would nevertheless be important information in carrying out a utilitarian calculation about the costs and benefits likely to follow the overriding of confidentiality.

More positive arguments for a right not to know are of both non-consequentialist and consequentialist sorts.

17

The human condition is one of limited knowledge

There is an argument that since the human condition is one of limited knowledge, it does not make sense to say that we ought to know, or that there is a duty to know (Jonas, quoted in Zimmerli, 1992). The objection to this argument is that it does not follow from the fact that the human condition is one of limited knowledge and that it is not possible that we should know everything, that there is a right not to know any particular thing where that knowledge is available.

Consequentialist arguments

Knowledge causes distress   One argument for the right not to know is the harm that can result from knowledge. A distinction is commonly drawn however between knowledge and its use, the idea being that knowledge in itself is morally neutral. In the context under discussion the application of this point would be that it is our attitude to genetic knowledge rather than the knowledge itself which is significant. How can knowledge itself be harmful? It can of course be shocking or upsetting. Sayings such as 'Where ignorance is bliss, 'tis folly to be wise'; 'What you don't know can't hurt you' bring out the point that knowledge may result in distress, though the degree to which this is the case is at least partly determined by the attitude we adopt to that knowledge.

From a consequentialist point of view, what has to be considered is whether the overall benefits of knowledge outweigh the disadvantages. The lack of knowledge can also cause harm: decisions taken in ignorance, in reproductive matters for example, have the potential to lead to harm that could have been avoided. Knowledge helps us to avoid bad outcomes and choose good ones.

Certain kinds of misery however, should perhaps be given special weighting. It may not be justifiable to take away hope from a person by exposing them to knowledge they do not want. Let us consider the case of a woman, shown on British television, who had a family history of premature Alzheimer's disease, who wondered about every instance of forgetfulness - aware that she was being watched for symptoms by her family - and who was offered a predictive test. A reason for refusing this test was that while she did not know, she had hope. Of course, the loss of hope is not an inevitable reaction. Some people may experience the knowledge as a liberation from the agony of uncertainty.

Other consequences for the individual Apart from the shock and unhappiness of coming to terms with an unpleasant diagnosis, genetic knowledge may have serious social consequences for the individual in terms of stigmatisation and discrimination. These however are strictly speaking arguments for restricting the access of others to the knowledge rather than for a right of the individual concerned not to know.

It is appropriate to consider the extent to which the considerations mentioned here also apply in other medical contexts - in other words, how far genetics

18

constitutes a special case. In medicine generally the presumption is that there is a right to a diagnosis, although the debate about disclosing the fact of terminal illness continues. The burden of proof is typically thought to rest with the professional, however, to justify non-disclosure, in terms of e.g. therapeutic privilege, rather than it being for the patient to justify a right not to know. But one special feature of genetic information that gives rise to a claim of a right not to know is its hiddenness - the information can and frequently does give rise to no symptoms, especially where what is at issue is a predisposition to a multifactorial condition. The person who is terminally ill has however normally (though not always) sought medical advice from a consciousness that something is wrong.

Autonomy and self-determination   What of the argument from self-determination? If the right to know is based on autonomy as expressed in a claim to self-determination, then perhaps the same argument can allow an individual to waive that right? If we understand autonomy in a wider sense, however, as empowerment, then the argument sounds rather different. To waive knowledge is to waive empowerment - is this a right? It might be argued that such a right conflicts with responsibility. On the other hand it might be argued that genetic knowledge is not empowering, at least not always, and that in some sense restriction of knowledge might be necessary to protect autonomy or an individual's sense of self.

Integrity/ sense of self   Some of the most interesting arguments concern this sense of self and notions of integrity and privacy. The Danish Council of Ethics has argued that although a justification of giving genetic information e.g. by genetic screening is empowerment, to give them 'scope for action' (Danish Council of Ethics, 1993, p. 50), there may come a point at which so much information is forthcoming that it may become an intrusion into the individual's private sphere, and at that point genetic screening is indefensible.

The concept of privacy here suggests a boundary around the self which should not be violated. It is not equivalent to self-determination - it is not saying that individuals should be able to do or have what they want, but making a point about the inviolability of the private sphere. Widmer speaks of the right to 'adopt and maintain a subjective image of oneself, which may objectively be false. I am not obliged to agree ... to receive information ... which could lead me to modify my picture of myself in an undesirable manner' (Widmer, 1994, p. 184). This point depends on the hiddenness of genetic information mentioned above. A woman who has a genetic predisposition to develop breast cancer in later life may have a self-image that is incompatible with this as a possible future. It might be argued that this example is unrealistic, because, given that breast cancer is multifactorial, every woman must acknowledge some risk, unless her image of her possible future is misguided. But some risks may be so remote as to seem virtually inconceivable. Genetics makes risks more or less probable. Is it

19

justifiable to intrude on this woman's self-perception? Is there more to this than the removal of hope? To what extent should the desire of an individual to retain a particular self-image take priority over other considerations?

There are arguments to suggest that the purported right not to know relies on an over-individualistic approach to the ethical issues. (Analogously, in the debates about the Human Genome Diversity Project, it may be asked whether a group's image of itself should remain unchallenged by discoveries about genetic closeness to other groups from whom they might regard themselves as very different). These arguments are to a considerable extent concerned with the notion of responsibility rather than rights.

Arguments against a right not to know

Solidarity and responsibility

The argument against such a right may be based on the value of solidarity. Kåre Berg suggests that 'Making vital information about one's genetic disorder available to persons with whom one shares genes is a highly ethical act of solidarity with one's own group' (Berg, 1994, p. 124). In order to carry out this act of solidarity, however, one has to have the information to share, which in turn suggests a responsibility to know it. To choose not to know is questionable if the knowledge has consequences for others. These consequences may be of importance both to persons currently alive who are making reproductive decisions and to as yet unborn generations.

An individual may not want to participate in a population screening programme because of a claimed right not to know. But this demonstrates lack of solidarity. Carlos-Maria Romeo-Casabona (1994) has argued that an individual who asserts a right not to know in some sense *already* knows that he or she is at risk and thus implies that a degree of self-deception is occurring. The point of the assertion is to prevent the greater certainty from adversely affecting personal and social well-being. Casabona's point is perhaps overstated, however, in the light of the possibility of broad spectrum population screening. There may be a case for making a distinction between different kinds of case - between those at the population level of risk and those in an 'at risk' category.

Public health

Walter Zimmerli (1990) has suggested that public health considerations provide an argument against a right not to know. The individual's self-image should perhaps give way before this. Widmer argues, however, that it is not sufficient to discuss at the theoretical level the merits of individualist concern for autonomy versus communitarianism with its value of solidarity. Society, in his view, has not yet accepted the idea of duties of solidarity in genetic research, and such duties must first be accepted by the individual: 'the establishment of a sense of responsibility in the society at large begins with awareness on the part of the individual' (Widmer, 1994, p. 187). The duty to participate cannot simply be imposed.

Conclusion

The recent move towards a more communitarian approach to ethics and medical ethics in particular has a special significance in genetics with its emphasis on relatedness. It has given rise to the suggestion that emphasis on individual rights should be supplemented if not replaced by consideration of individual responsibilities. Then concern for individual confidentiality and privacy would be at the very least mediated by responsibility to share genetic knowledge, which in turn implies a responsibility to know it. It might be argued, however, that the responsibility one has to one's partner and family is of a different kind from one's responsibility to institutions and employers, just as their respective needs to know are different. This at least points the way forward, to consideration of the extent of the feasibility and desirability of solidarity in genetics. Although this issue is one small part of the domain of morality, the arguments about why the individual should show solidarity are analogous to the arguments about the 'Why should I be moral?' question. Widmer's suggestion that duties of solidarity must first be accepted by the individual are reminiscent of Philippa Foot's argument that morality is a system of hypothetical imperatives supported by a band of 'volunteers' (Foot, 1978). Although there are good arguments for displaying solidarity, in the light of the potential for adverse psychological effects of imposing unwanted knowledge and uncertainty about how people will in fact use information that they have, it is difficult to be confident about its feasibility in practice. What would be required as a preliminary would be the *desire* to show solidarity in matters of genetics, arising from increased public awareness of the issues.

In addition to these general theoretical and practical considerations, however, there are reasons to think that different approaches may be appropriate for different types of case. The relevance of the difference between the population level of risk and an 'at risk' category has been mentioned. Whether the genetic information is relevant to a reproductive decision or the future health care management of an individual is another factor. The nature of the particular condition may also be relevant. All of these factors point towards the conclusion that there is a simple opposition neither between a right to know and a right not to know, nor between a right to know and a duty to know.

References

Berg, K. (1994), 'The Need for Laws, Rules and Good Practices to Secure Optimal Disease Control', in *Ethics and Human Genetics,* pp. 122-134, Council of Europe: Strasbourg.

Chadwick, R. and Ngwena, C. (1995), 'The Human Genome Project, Predictive Testing and Insurance Contracts: Ethical and Legal Responses', *Res Publica,* Vol. 1, No. 2, pp. 115-129.

Danish Council of Ethics (1993), *Ethics and the Mapping of the Human Genome,* Danish Council of Ethics: Copenhagen.

Foot, P. (1978), 'Morality as a System of Hypothetical Imperatives' in Foot, P. *Virtues and Vices,* pp. 157-73, Blackwell: Oxford.

Harper, P.S. (1992), 'Genetic Testing and Insurance', *Journal of the Royal College of Physicians of London,* Vol. 26, No. 2, pp. 184-187.

Kielstein, R. and Sass, H.M. (1992), 'Right not to Know or Duty to Know? Prenatal Screening for Polycystic Renal Disease', *Journal of Medicine and Philosophy,* No. 17, pp. 395-405.

Laird, L. et al. (1996), 'Neonatal Screening for Sickle Cell Disorders: what About the Carrier Infants?', *British Medical Journal,* No. 7054, pp. 407-11.

Ngwena, C. and Chadwick, R. (1993), 'Genetic Diagnostic Information and the Duty of Confidentiality: Ethics and Law', *Medical Law International,* No. 1, pp. 73-95.

Romeo-Casabona, C.M. (1994), 'Human Rights Issues in Research on Medical Genetics', in *Ethics and Human Genetics,* pp. 167-174, Council of Europe: Strasbourg.

Royal College of Physicians, (1991), *Ethical Issues in Clinical Genetics,* Royal College of Physicians: London.

Stone, D.H. and Stewart, S. (1996), 'Screening and the New Genetics: A Public Health Perspective on the Ethical Debate', *Journal of Public Health Medicine,* Vol. 18, No. 1, pp. 3-5.

Widmer, P. (1994), 'Human Rights Issues in Research on Medical Genetics', in *Ethics and Human Genetics*, pp. 175-188, Council of Europe: Strasbourg.

Zimmerli, W.Ch. (1990), 'Who has the Right to Know the Genetic Constitution of a Particular Person?' in Chadwick, D. et al., *Human Genetic Information: Science, Law and Ethics,* pp. 93-102, John Wiley: Chichester.

2 Individual rights and genetics: the historical perspective

A comment on Ruth Chadwick's paper

Urban Wiesing

I intend to look at the same issue as the previous paper from a different perspective; the historical one. The two reasons with which I justify this change of perspective are, first, that implicitly or explicitly we are always arguing from historical evidence; and second, that genetics has a history which is worth telling - especially in reference to individual rights.

Before starting to look at the history of genetics, I would like to examine the way in which historical evidence should be used in a moral discourse. I will therefore clarify the relationship between historical knowledge and moral decisions in a general way at the theoretical level. So the first part of my article contains theoretical considerations, the second part tries to look at the history of genetics within this framework.

The relevance of historical evidence for moral decisions

To a certain extent ethical arguments are unavoidably based on historical arguments. We use historical examples to support a moral decision or to warn us; we refer to historically proven values or norms, and we refer to developments of history to clarify the origin of a moral problem and sometimes, allegedly, to find a solution. A careful look at moral discussions - especially in medicine - confirms that without historical arguments our linguistics would be much more limited and we could use only a small proportion of our common terms.

But do we always use historical arguments in a justifiable manner? Or, to put the question more generally, how can we use historical arguments properly? In order to answer that question a distinction must be made between history in the sense of 'development of events' and history in the sense of 'story'. To overlook that distinction would evoke confusion.

A connection between history in the sense of 'development of events' and moral decisions cannot be justified, because a convincing theory of the development of events would be required. But since the two most substantial theories, that is the teleology of conscience in German Idealism and the teleology of society in Marxism, are strongly criticised by plausible arguments, such a theory of the development of events is supposed to be 'unknowable' (Marquard, 1992). A convincing theory of the development of events does not exist. To use a fashionable term: history is chaotic. We do not know the laws of the development of events, nor can we predict the future. And due to this lack of historical laws, we cannot derive moral laws from the development of events.

On the other hand, the hope of finding in history 'timeless values' or 'metahistorical norms' (which would ease the moral decision enormously, because they only have to be known) must fail if one is methodologically honest. It is simply impossible to find timeless values by looking at former times, by looking at the past. A theory that promises to find such values or norms will surely be undermined. That means that a mandatory connection between the development of events and moral decisions cannot be justified. A philosophy of history can neither be a surrogate nor a basic foundation of moral philosophy.

But the more important and more interesting question seems to be whether and in which way history, in the sense of 'stories' about the past, can influence a moral decision. So the question is: how may the products of historians - that means: stories about the past - justifiably influence moral decisions? It should be clear that a moral decision cannot be drawn exclusively from historical evidence, it cannot be drawn exclusively from stories about the past. But is it possible to make a moral decision without knowing the relevant history? The answer is: yes, it is possible, but it is unlikely that the resulting decision is a prudent one.

This thesis can be explained by looking at the four tasks of ethics and at the role of historical evidence in each task. According to the German philosopher Birnbacher (1993) ethics has four tasks: analysis, criticism, construction, moral pragmatics. It is simply impossible to analyse a moral problem without knowing the relevant past and the historical precedents. It is hardly possible to criticise moral decisions without referring to the past either positively or negatively. And if we look at the main task of ethics, the construction of moral norms, we will see that some prominent theories of contemporary ethics refer to moral convictions that are historically given, widely accepted, and historically proved; they are using the reconstructive approach as it came to be called. I think that the most popular theory of bioethics, principlism (see Beauchamp and Childress, 1994, Gillon, 1993), is an example of a reconstructive approach. The same is true of Wolfgang Wieland's theory of medical ethics which is widely discussed in Germany (1986). It is obviously impossible to neglect the history if a reconstructive approach is used that begins with historically given moral convictions. Last but not least, in moral pragmatics it is often useful to consider former regulations which are proved to fulfil the pragmatic needs.

Thus historical evidence can make us aware of crucial developments, can make us cautious, can make us sensitive, realistic, and hence more prudent. And in a reconstructive approach historical 'givens' provide the point from which it is to start.

But we must look at the character of stories to understand the way in which historical arguments deriving from stories about the past may be used in ethics. Stories about the past can be written in different ways. History must necessarily be interpreted, and there is not a one and only true interpretation of history. Therefore using historical evidence in ethics is always a question of interpretation. In this sense history is a readable text (Fellmann, 1991), a text worth reading for moral discourse. However, when a single case is to be decided, historical evidence will always be vague. Historical evidence only serves to provide general guidance.

That means: historical arguments are always weak arguments in ethics. But a weak argument is better than no argument. And many weak arguments supporting the same idea may become a strong argument. With that theoretical clarification let us now look at the history of genetics and its moral impacts (see Wiesing, 1995).

The history of genetics

Ruth Chadwick has written about the conflicts between different persons' right to know and not to know. I want to focus on the fact that she was mainly concerned with individual rights and not the rights of society. This emphasis is not self-evident, but a historically given result, one that can even be historically justified, as I will explain.

A look at the history of genetics shows us some applications of genetics that are considered to be morally sound and others that are considered to be morally wrong, sometimes even morally disastrous. It is neither the knowledge nor the approach nor the technology of genetics itself that is deemed immoral, but certain applications. What, however, were the circumstances that turned those applications immoral? The answer to that question would require an overview of the whole history of genetics, therefore I will focus on the most tragic example in that history - genetics during the Nazi era in Germany.

Genetics during the Nazi era

This era in genetics is considered immoral because of the following special features:

1   The physicians in Germany during the Nazi era were obligated primarily to the collective benefit, more precisely: the future benefit of the race, and only secondarily to the individual benefit. 'Your nation is everything and you are nothing' - that was the official maxim of German medicine at that time (Toellner, 1989).

2   Before and during the Nazi era the politicians wanted to solve social problems via medicine. The complex social and psychological phenomena were reduced to one cause and treated with only one strategy, the genetic approach. Genetics became the primary science for solving social problems and the plurality of approaches was lost. By referring to genetics there was a tendency to medicalise the social tensions which followed rapid industrialisation (Weingart, Kroll and Bayertz, 1988).

3   The science of genetics divided the population into normal and abnormal members, not only in a descriptive, but also in a normative sense. The geneticist did not reflect on that categorisation. The methodological honesty of science was simply forgotten as scientists, physicians, and politicians used scientific knowledge to transform political decisions into 'scientific' decisions.

4   Finally, human rights and patient rights were heavily violated.

I suspect that an examination of the applications of genetics in other countries would bring similar results: under the circumstances mentioned before the use of genetics is judged to be immoral.

Guidance from the history of genetics

Considering the theoretical restriction on using historical evidence the history of genetics may give us the following advice:

1   It should always be clear what scientific knowledge is able to answer and what it cannot answer; namely political and moral decisions.

2   It should always be clear, that the genetic approach is only one approach and not the only one to cope with genetic diseases. Other approaches should be offered. The individual should always have the right not to use genetics and the right not to know genetic information but to cope with disease in other ways.

3   Human rights and patient rights should be carefully maintained in the face of options created by new technologies.

4   The individual benefit, rather than the collective benefit, should always be the main and overriding consideration. Genetics should not be used to solve social problems but to ease individual pain and prevent or cure individual diseases. The patient-physician-relationship with its confidentiality and devotion towards the single patient must be protected, and genetics should

always be applied within that relationship. Medicine should be strictly individual. And the right to know or not to know is an individual right.

Therefore the history of genetics supports an approach which emphasises a very strong personal right to know and the right not to know despite all the difficulties Ruth Chadwick mentioned in her article. I cannot solve the problem of balancing individual rights, but, from the historical point of view I can only underline that the question is how to balance individual rights, and not how to restrict them in favour of potential collective benefits. The single patient, his or her welfare and his or her will should be the point for all considerations. The historical evidence supports individual rights that are heavily protected, a medicine that is orientated towards the individual, a protected physician-patient-relationship and a variation of approaches.

References

Beauchamp, T.L., Childress, J.F. (1994), (4th ed.), *Principles of Biomedical Ethics*, Oxford University Press: New York ,Oxford.

Birnbacher, D. (1993), 'Welche Ethik ist als Bioethik tauglich?', in Ach, J.S. and Gaidt, A. (ed.), *Herausforderung der Bioethik*, pp. 45-67, Frommann-Holzboog: Stuttgart-Bad Cannstatt.

Fellmann, F. (1991), 'Geschichte als Text. Ein Plädoyer für die Geschichtsphilosophie', *Information Philosophie*, No. 4, pp. 5-14.

Gillon, R. (1993), (ed.), *Principles of Health Care Ethics*, John Wiley and Sons: Chichester, New York, Brisbane, Toronto, Singapore.

Marquard, O. (1982), *Schwierigkeiten mit der Geschichtsphilosophie*, Aufsätze, Suhrkamp: Frankfurt a.M.

Toellner, R. (1989), 'Ärzte im Dritten Reich', *Deutsches Ärzteblatt*, Vol. 86, pp. C. 1427-1433.

Weingart, P., Kroll, J. and Bayertz, K. (1988), *Rasse, Blut und Gene. Geschichte der Eugenik und Rassenhygiene in Deutschland*, Suhrkamp: Frankfurt a.M.

Wieland, W. (1986), *Strukturwandel der Medizin und ärztliche Ethik. Philosophische Überlegungen zu Grundfragen einer praktischen Wissenschaft*, Carl Winter Universitätsverlag: Heidelberg.

Wiesing, U. (1995), 'Zum Verhältnis von Geschichte und Ethik in der Medizin', *Internationale Zeitschrift für Geschichte und Ethik der Naturwissenschaften, Technik und Medizin*, neue Serie, Vol. 3, pp. 129-144.

3 Sociological perspectives on the right to know and the right not to know

Mairi Levitt

Introduction

With the mapping of the human genome not yet complete and news stories on genetic breakthroughs regularly appearing, it might seem perverse to be writing about the right not to know. Genetic stories are news in a way that stories about other causes of disease are not, unless a new angle can be found. Just as geneticists will focus on the genetic component of diseases, disorders and behaviour sociologists will focus on the social, political, economic and cultural components. The differing theoretical perspectives can lead to radically different policies; for example, if IQ is largely determined by genetic inheritance then a differentiated education system might be favoured, rather than an egalitarian one, on the grounds that 'if the differences really are inborn, there is no use forcing children beyond their capabilities'[1] (Goodhart, 1994, p. 51). A sociologist could agree with Goodhart when he argues that there are ideological reasons why people favour environmental/social explanations of differences in children's abilities, but would add that equally there are ideological reasons for favouring genetic explanations of differences in abilities, behaviour and disease. The purpose of this chapter is to look at the implications of 'geneticization' for the roles of individuals, professionals and societies in health care. Throughout the discussion of genetic screening and testing it has to be remembered that the purpose of the programmes is to provide some benefits for individuals/families and/or society which have to be weighed against any disadvantages or individual and social costs.

Exercising control over your health

In countries with a liberal democratic tradition, to be a full member of society, a citizen, is to be able to exercise rational choice and control over one's own life. In the area of health, the emphasis in health campaigns, women's magazines and advertising in the UK has been on the individual making the right choices and taking control; knowledge is assumed to be empowering. Individuals are urged to get in control of their bodies by exercise and diet. Some current advertising slogans with this theme are:

'Help your heart stay healthy' - an advertisement for garlic in pill form
'Drink it to your heart's content'- fruit juice containing soluble fibre
'If you would like to give your body a little extra help' - advertising mineral and vitamin supplements

These are commercial companies selling a product to consumers so it would be naive to expect anything other than an address to individuals portrayed as in control of their health. For those with the economic means health and the body are viewed as increasingly under individual control to be shaped in accordance with one's chosen lifestyle which will include appropriate consumption (Bunton and Burrows, 1995).

The individualisation of responsibility for health provides an explanation for death in societies where life expectancy is high. If someone dies at a time considered to be premature it is not long before those hearing the news consider the reasons for this early death; perhaps the person smoked, drank alcohol excessively, was overweight, did not go for regular screening, ignored early warning signs or overworked and suffered from stress. If one or more of these individual and avoidable factors can be linked to the death those left behind feel themselves to be more secure, particularly if they happen to be slim, non-smokers who drink moderately! Developments in genetics might seem to remove responsibility from the individual; if the trait is 'in the family'. However, the onus is now on the individual to gather information on their genetic inheritance and take appropriate action such as avoiding the birth of a child with the disorder.

Problems and solutions presented in the media

Being a responsible adult includes the duty to be proactive in health care and the media provide a major source of information, as discussed in chapter 8 (Chadwick and Levitt). While advertising can link the problem and the solution in a simple equation (Dandruff? Not if you use product X) consumers know that reality will be less clear-cut. When reporting medical advances the same certainty may be apparent in the early stages when the only information is from the researchers concerned but 'consumers' will find it more difficult$_2$ to question or reject, say, a genetic screening test, than a brand of shampoo. Could the health care system actually cope with millions of patients demanding adequate information and exercising choices? A father was jailed for two and a half years and the mother given probation following the death of their child in a diabetic coma. The parents' account was that they wanted to discuss the insulin treatment before their child began injections; 'parents have a right to know the options in order to give informed consent' (The Times, 22.11.94). Their questions about insulin, including whether it was made from animal products and if there were alternatives were cited as evidence of religious zealotry. The hospital made great efforts to contact the couple after they left the hospital in order to begin treatment. The merits of such a case cannot be ascertained from a newspaper article but the implication is that parents do not normally demand such information before treatment begins. This leads to a suspicion that the 'right to know' is trumpeted in some circumstances rather than others; in particular during pregnancy.

Mothers-to-be are 'encouraged to select every aspect of their lifestyle during pregnancy, their ante-natal care and delivery of their baby' under the Informed Choice initiative. The advice given is based on the 'latest medical research and good practice, not on old wives' tales, personal opinion, hospital policy or what is most convenient for the doctor or midwife' (The Daily Express, 16.1.96). What is defined as the latest research and good practice is constantly changing, over recommended sleeping positions for infants for example, but women who base choices on their own values, religious tradition or advice of relatives will probably be thought not to be making an informed choice unless their choice is seen as a reasonable one.

The role of the professional

If patients exercise the right not to know, it has been suggested that they would be imposing a burden on their doctor instead of taking responsibility for the choice themselves (John Harris in reply to Jørgen Husted, Turku, 1995).[3] However, the medical profession will frequently, or usually, have more knowledge than their patient about the meaning of test results or his or her prognosis. It is not obvious that information on, say, the sex of a baby after amniocentesis or the result of a test for a genetic disorder, which a woman chooses not to know, would be a burden on her General Practitioner for whom she is one patient on a list of thousands. This may sound like a call for a return to paternalism, when the doctor decided what was best for the patient to know but the doctor has never told patients all the known risk factors, only selected ones. For example, the GP is unlikely to inform a mother from social class five of the (statistically) greater risks of her baby dying in the first year of life, but might talk about the risk to the baby if she smokes. One group of risks is due to a combination of social, cultural, economic and environmental factors over which the mother has little control and is difficult to quantify for one specific individual. The other seems to be within the power of the individual to do something about, although also linked to specific social, economic and environmental factors. Information about a genetic disorder may fit into either of these types of risk.

The idea that a service on offer by the medical profession might not be desirable is a new one, in the UK anyway. Doctors have enjoyed high status and the trust of their patients. Social attitudes surveys in the UK record a high degree of satisfaction with general practitioners which has changed little over the last ten years despite increasing dissatisfaction with other aspects of the health service (Jowell, Curtice, Brook and Advendt, 1994, p. 58). Davidson, McIntyre and Smith, commentating on the social impact of testing for susceptibility to common chronic diseases, write 'The idea that knowing about possible futures may actually decrease the quality of a person's life is not easily accommodated within the essentially rationalist or utilitarian philosophy underlying the idea of screening' (Davison, Macintyre and Smith, 1994, pp. 353-354).

Benefits and disbenefits

The United Nations Declaration of Human Rights Article 27(1) states that 'Everyone has the right freely to participate in the cultural life of the community, and to enjoy the arts *and to share in scientific advancement and its benefits*' (my emphasis). The assumption is that scientific advancement and benefits go together whereas public figures are more cautious about talking of advancements in other areas of cultural life. Public opinion surveys show that the general public, students and those with scientific qualifications have similar views on the benefits and risks of science and technology; commenting on his International Bioethics Survey, Darryl Macer concludes that 'you cannot educate people not to see any risks' (Macer, 1994, p. 82) .

It may seem odd for a social scientist to see any need to defend the right not to know since sociological research has attempted to make people aware of inequalities in areas such as education, health and life chances in general. Underlying this work is the assumption that such inequalities are wrong. This research highlights inequalities between groups with particular social characteristics and it focuses attention on the social causes with the potential for change. Some genetic screening programmes have performed a similar function in that they revealed the extent of a genetic disorder in a definable group and did something to mitigate the effects of the disorder by accepting it as a group/community problem e.g. screening for carriers of Tay Sachs and thalassemia. However genetic testing may reveal the inevitable fate of an individual; this boy will develop muscular dystrophy if he lives through infancy whatever we do; or, in the case of a multifactorial disease, like breast cancer, genetic testing may reveal a high probability of developing the disease. It is probably more accurate to say it will confirm the risk since women will already suspect that their risk is high because of relatives affected with the disease. In these examples, the focus on genetics individualises the disorder making it an insoluble individual or family problem. However, in the case of breast cancer, estimates are that only five to ten per cent of the total cases can be said to be inherited (New Scientist, 10.12.94, p. 4) whereas, according to the World Health Organisation, 80-90 per cent of all cancer cases are caused by environmental factors (Vågerö, 1995, p. 14).

Exercising the right to know

Families affected by a specific disorder may have a more optimistic view of genetic testing. The Genetic Interest Group (GIG) representing voluntary organisations concerned with genetic disorders, considers that genetic services offer people 'the potential to acquire information about their genetic make-up ... [which] though it might be bad news, at least allows them to plan out their lives and make informed reproductive decisions' (Genetic Interest Group, 1995, p. 3). Displaying an impatience with a cautious approach to the genetic testing of children GIG criticised the Clinical Genetics Society Report as 'overly preoccupied with psychological considerations and the harm that knowledge of genetic disorders can cause within families' (Dalby, 1995, p. 490). If those with immediate experience of genetic disorders want screening services why should others be concerned about the right not to know?

There is, of course, a difference between targeted screening programmes for families or particular ethnic groups with experience of a specific disorder and the routine screening of, say, pregnant women. While the former will reassure individuals or confirm what they already feared, the latter creates fears and then reassures some women, a proportion of whom will be falsely reassured (Rothenberg and Thomson 1994). Once screening programmes become routine the element of informed consent will diminish, as it has done with ultrasound in pregnancy and the PKU test. As the House of Commons Report on human genetics and its consequences noted 'Any screening programme should be carefully evaluated before its introduction. However there appears to be no mechanism to ensure that this is the case' (House of Commons, 1995, para. 98).

Coping with risk

Whereas in health education campaigns the correct course of action is clear; take these (easy) steps and you will reduce your risk, risk management for those with a genetic disorder may involve all aspects of life from the type of employment, leisure activities, reproductive plans but still could not avoid the inevitable end stage of the disease, for example, in the case of polycystic kidney disease (Kielstein and Sass, 1992).

In pregnancy, however carefully the results of a screening test are explained and the estimated risk of having a child with a particular disorder conveyed to the mother, it does not relate to the experience of having a child. The child either will or will not have Down's whether the estimated risk after a serum screening test is 1 in 1,200 or 1 in 7.

In Parsons and Atkinson's study of women in families with Duchenne Muscular Dystrophy, many of the women had resolved the state of being 'at risk' by adopting 'categorical recipes for knowledge and action. The probabilistic was expressed as a matter of certainty ... I can only have girls' (1992, p. 454-446). The women translated their risk into 'everyday recipes for reproductive action that could be readily incorporated into their personal stocks of knowledge' (1992, p.454). To see this process as a product of misunderstanding on the part of the women is to miss the point. A carrier couple of the cystic fibrosis or thalassemia gene might be able to recall the textbook risk of any child they have being a carrier or suffering from the disorder, perhaps complete with the diagram of four box and circle shaped children two of whom are carriers and one a sufferer. What they want to know is whether if they become pregnant the baby will be affected or not; a certainty which only the availability of preimplantation screening can come close to providing.

Conclusions

Individuals are expected to take responsibility for their health, but these rational autonomous individuals are assumed to be people with the opportunity and resources to exercise choice and to be in control of their lives (and for mothers, their children's lives as well). Those who lack the opportunity or ability to exercise rational choice and make long term plans include the homeless and the poor who are excluded from full citizenship with its rights and duties. Their health, and that of their families, would be better served by resources directed to reducing socio-economic inequality than by the extension of routine genetic screening with attendant risks of stigma, uninsurability, stress and lack of acceptable treatment (Wilkins, 1994, Smith and Morris, 1994, Shickle and Chadwick, 1994). However, measures to reduce inequality are less likely to advance scientific and technical knowledge, provide commercial opportunities or international kudos. Should state funded health services say 'no' to routine screening programmes, although commercial screening by post will be increasingly available for those who want it and can afford it? For example, Cystic Fibrosis testing by post for £94 with telephone counselling on the implications of a positive result (The Times, 19.7.95). Technology cannot be uninvented and, in any case, any form of rationing or paternalism (you should not have this information) does not fit in with the stress on openness and patient's rights in the health service. Genetic screening brings undoubted benefits particularly for those who already know they, or any children they may have, are at risk, but undoubted pressures and new dilemmas for those caught up in programmes offering diagnosis, with varying degrees of certainty, and treatment with uncertain benefits or termination of a pregnancy.

In reality the right to know is not freely or completely exercised although it is frequently evoked both by medical professionals and pressure groups. The right not to know becomes a topic for debate as the technology to predict risks for individuals runs ahead of both available treatments and the human ability to cope with such knowledge.

Notes

1   Assuming that IQ measures intelligence and that intelligence is the crucial factor in academic success.
2   This does not mean that the media are necessarily distorting the words of the researchers concerned - reports in the quality press of *new* techniques are often similar to those in *New Scientist* and more specialised journals with the addition of quotes from appropriate experts and a catchy headline. See examples in chapter 8.
3   Elsewhere Professor John Harris has argued that it is doubtful that there is, or could be, a right to remain in ignorance or 'a general obligation to tell all, in all circumstances' but there is 'an obligation to tell all to those who wish to be told' (Harris, J. 1985, *The Value of Life,* Routledge: London, pp. 208f.

References

Bindless, L. (1996), 'Individualism v Communitarianism: Ethics of Breast Cancer Screening: The Need for a New Approach' Parker, M. (ed.), *Ethics and Community. Proceedings of the 1995 Conference of the Centre for Professional Ethics,* University of Central Lancashire, pp. 301-314.
Bunton, R. and Burrows, R. (1995), 'Consumption and Health in the "Epidemiological" Clinic of Late Modern Medicine', Bunton, R., Nettleton, S. and Burrows, R. (eds), *The Sociology of Health Promotion* Routledge, London, chapter 16.
Chadwick, R. and Levitt, M. (1994), 'Mass Media and Public Discussion in Bioethics'. Unpublished paper presented at *International Association of Bioethics 11 World Congress*, 24-26 October 1994, Buenos Aires: Argentina.
Dalby, S. (1995), 'GIG Response to the UK Clinical Genetics Society Report "The Genetic Testing of Children", *Journal of Medical Genetics,* Vol. 32, pp. 490-494.

Davidson, C., Macintyre, S. and Smith, G.D. (1994), 'The Potential Social Impact of Predictive Genetic Testing for Susceptibility to Common Chronic Diseases: A Review and Proposed Research Agenda', *Sociology of Health and Illness,* Vol. 16, No. 3, pp. 340-371.

Jowell, R., Curtice, J., Brook, L. and Ahrendt, D., (eds), (1994), *British Social Attitudes. The 11th Report, 1994/1995 Edition,* Dartmouth Publishing: England.

Genetic Interest Group (1995), *The Present Organisation of Genetic Services in the United Kingdom,* Genetic Interest Group: London.

Kielstein, R.and Sass, H.M. (1992), 'Right not to Know or Duty to Know?'. Prenatal Screening for Polycystic Renal Disease', *Journal of Medicine and Philosophy,* Vol. 17, pp. 395-405.

Macer, D. (1994), *Bioethics for the People by the People,* Eubios Ethics Institute, Christchurch: New Zealand.

Parsons, E. and Atkinson, P. (1992), 'Lay Constructions of Genetic Risk', *Sociology of Health and Illness,* Vol. 14, no. 4, pp. 437-455.

Rothenberg, K.H. and Thomson, E.J. (eds), (1994), *Women and Prenatal Testing - Facing the Challenges of Genetic Technology,* Ohio State University Press: Columbia.

Science and Technology Committee, House of Commons (1995), *Human Genetics: The Science and its Consequences,* Third Report, Vol. 1, Report and Minutes of Proceedings, HMSO: London.

Shickle, D. and Chadwick, R. (1994) 'The Ethics of Screening: Is "Screeningitis" an Incurable Disease?', *Journal of Medical Ethics,* Vol. 20, pp. 12-18.

Smith, G.D. and Morris, J. (1994), 'Increasing Inequalities in the Health of the Nation', *British Medical Journal,* Vol. 309, pp. 1453-1454.

Vågerö, D. (1995), 'Health Inequalities as Policy Issues - Reflection on Ethics, Policy and Public Health', *Sociology of Health and Illness,* Vol. 17, No. 1, pp. 1-19.

Wilkins, R.G. (1994), 'Divided we Fall. The Poor Pay the Price of Increased Social Inequality with Their Health', *British Medical Journal,* Vol. 308, pp. 1113-1114.

4   The meaning of 'rights' in the right to know debate

Ingmar Pörn

Before I turn to the question of how to interpret the right to access and not to access genetic information about oneself I will set the stage by telling a frame story about rights and some related matters. This story is developed only to the extent required for letting some of the complexities emerge.

W.N. Hohfeld divided the class of rights (jural relations) into two sub-groups, one comprising claims (rights *stricto sensu*), duties, privileges and no-claims, the other powers, liabilities, immunities and disabilities. The former compel, forbid or permit conduct, the latter are legally defined abilities to bring about a change in legal relations.[1]

Rights in the first group may be regarded as bundles of normative positions. So-called simple one-agent normative positions with respect to a state of affairs S may be defined in terms of the deontic modality Shall ('It shall be the case that'), negation - ('It is not the case that'), and the agency construction E(A,S) ('A brings it about that S'). The definitions run as follows:

Table 4.1
Simple one-agent normative positions

Types	Definiens:
obligation	ShallE(A,S)
counter-obligation	ShallE(A,-S)
prohibition	Shall-E(A,S)
counter-prohibition	Shall-E(A,-S)
freedom	-ShallE(A,-S)
counter-freedom	-ShallE(A,S)
permission	-Shall-E(A,S)
counter-permission	-Shall-E(A,-S)

More complex one-agent positions are defined as consistent conjunction of one-agent positions. For example, the conjunction of a permission and a counter-permission (with respect to one and the same state of affairs) is consistent, whereas the conjunction of an obligation and a counter-obligation is inconsistent and, therefore, it does not define a complex one-agent position. In order to determine the consistent conjunctions, the logical relationships between one-agent positions must be taken into account. These are exhibited in the diagrams below (where the arrow stands for implication).

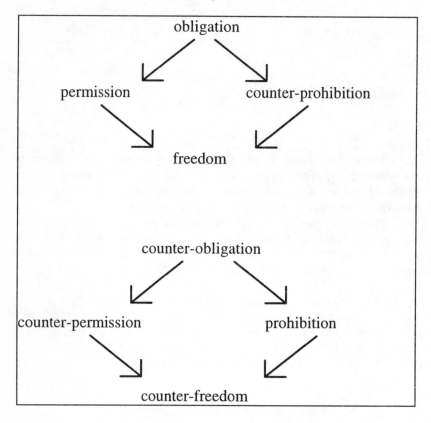

Figure 4.1   **Entailments between simple one-agent normative positions**

The consistent conjunctions may be tabulated as follows.

Table 4.2
Complex one-agent normative positions

	obligation	counter-obligation	prohibition	counter-prohibition
1	+	-	-	+
2	-	+	+	-
3	-	-	+	+
4	-	-	+	-
5	-	-	-	+
6	-	-	-	-

For example, line 3 represents the conjunction:

> not obligation (= counter-freedom) and not counter-obligation (= freedom) and prohibition and counter-prohibition,

Since prohibition implies counter-freedom and counter-prohibition implies freedom, the list may be reduced to:

> prohibition and counter-prohibition,

Next we move into the field of two-agent normative positions. Instead of considering the normative positions of two agents severally, we can consider them in relation to each other with respect to one and the same state of affairs. It is within this perspective that rights in Hohfeld's first group arise.

Assume that S is a state of affairs involving A or B or both, for example the state of affairs that A has access to his or her genetic profile. What distributions of normative positions are possible with A and B as occupants or holders of these positions? A distribution allocating obligation to A to bring it about that he or she has access and obligation to B to bring it about that A does not have access is not feasible, but a distribution assigning permission to A and prohibition to B surely is feasible.

The first pair in Hohfeld's scheme is that of rights *stricto sensu* and duties or, as we have already said, claims and duties. According to Hohfeld, claims and duties are correlative, which means that A has a right of type claim against B in regard to S if and only if B has a duty against A in regard to S. More formally, Claim (A,B,S) if and only if Duty (B,A,S). In modern logical terminology, B's duty is the inverse of A's claim.

How should B's duty be understood? The answer is obvious: B's duty is his or her obligation to bring about S in the system of conjoint distributions of normative positions between A and B with respect to S.

The other pair of correlatives in Hohfeld's first group is that of privileges and no-claims. This means, if we read Hohfeld closely, that A's privilege against B with respect to S amounts to B having no counter-claims against A with respect to S. In other words, Privilege (A,B,) if and only if it is not the case that Counter-claim (B,A,S). The latter means that -ShallE (A,-S), which is A's normative position of type freedom, again in the system conjoint distributions of normative positions between A and B.

The other sub-group of rights and Hohfeld's analysis also comprises two pairs of correlatives (inverses), namely

powers	————————	liabilities
immunities	————————	disabilities

or, in other words,

Power (A,B,S) if and only if Liability (B,A,S)
Immunity (A,B,S) if and only if Disability (B,A,S)

For the interpretation of these the modality Can ('It can be the case that') may be used - it takes the place of Shall in the first sub-group. Power (A,B,S) is defined to mean CanE (A,S,). A good example is the power to make a will. A's power against B to make a will in which B is specified is a legally defined ability to alter B's legal conditions. When A has this power B is subject to the liability of having his or her legal conditions altered. The inverse of A's counter-power, CanE (A,-S), is of course B's counter-liability. Immunity (A,B,S) is defined as B's disability to bring it about that -S, in other words as -CanE (B,-S), and counter-immunity in A as against B as -CanE (B,S).[2]

Let us now turn to the question how the right to know and not to know might be understood. If we use the indicated framework for rights, it is evident that we have to answer the following questions in order to characterise the right:

1   how should the state of affairs be specified?
2   what is the type of the right, i.e. what are its normative and power components?
3   who are the parties involved?

Question 1 pertains to the state of affairs that is common to the normative position of the right - others appear in the appurtenant powers.

Two answers to question 1 immediately suggest themselves, namely:

1.1   the state of the affairs that A has access to genetic information about himself or herself
1.2   the state of affairs that A receives genetic information about himself or herself

40

The meaning intended in the former case is that A knows a method or procedure for obtaining the information, not necessarily that he or she actually obtains it. So understood 1.1 is clearly distinct from 1.2. In spite of this, the following normative positions may be advanced for both specifications:

For A: permission and counter-permission
For B: prohibition and counter-prohibition

In other words, free choice for A and prohibition for B to interfere. When the whole matter is seen from A's point of view, the prohibition for B is A's claim that B abstains from interfering, and A's free choice is his or her privilege against B with respect to abstaining from accessing or not accessing his or her own genetic information or receiving or not receiving it.

The main argument for this interpretation is an argument for autonomy and integrity. Free choice nicely reflects the idea of autonomy or self-determination. Prohibition for other parties reflects the idea of personal integrity in the sense of a territory or domain into which the agency of others is not allowed to enter.[3]

If A's normative positions of the right to know and not to know are understood in this way, the appurtenant powers will have to include his or her power to place himself or herself under the obligation to disclose the relevant data to some designated agency, and the power to place the same or some other agency under the obligation to register and store it, and of course the power to place somebody under the obligation to access the information from the register for A.[4] These are obvious if case A exercises his or her free choice by choosing to get access to or actually receive the information. The alternative choice is similarly attended by a set of powers.

This interpretation may be defended as a general rule while allowing for exceptions. If, for example, A is a patient and B his or her physician, there may be a case for giving the physician free choice as well - in the exercise of his or her competence he or she should be free to decide on the appropriateness of imparting or withholding information as a measure of care. This situation is of considerable interest because it shows that it is possible to have autonomy (of the kind defined above) without integrity (again as defined above).[5]

Notes

1 The original source is Hohfeld (1913). For logically oriented expositions see Kanger, S. and Kanger, H. (1966), Lindahl, L. (1977), Pörn, I. (1970), and Kanger, H. (1984). An interesting exposition of Hohfeld intended for readers in jurisprudence is Dias, (1964).

2 For clarifying observations on the relations between rights of the two sub-groups, see Dias, R.W.M (1964) and Tapper, C.F.H. (1973).

3 For integrity in this sense, cf The Danish Council of Ethics, (1993), pp. 13-16.
4 The Danish Council of Ethics, (1993), p. 11, makes a useful distinction between disclosure, registration, storage and dissemination of information. Dissemination raises issues other than the one discussed in this paper.
5 Ost, D.E. (1984) interprets the relation between the patient and the physician differently since he or she claims that the patient has a duty to receive the information and, hence, that the physician has a claim against the patient with respect to his or her receiving the information.   This interpretation presumably reflects a radically different understanding of the whole issue of the right not to know as compared with the position tentatively advanced in this paper.

References

Danish Council of Ethics (1993), *Ethics and the Mapping of the Human Genome*, The Danish Council of Ethics: Copenhagen.
Dias, R. W. M. (1964), (2nd ed.), *Jurisprudence*, Butherworths: London.
Hohfeld, W.N. (1913), 'Some Fundamental Legal Conceptions as Applied in Judicial Reasoning', *Yale Law Journal*, Vol. 23, pp. 16-59.
Kanger, S. and Kanger, H. (1966), 'Rights and Parliamentarism', *Theoria*, Vol. 32, pp. 85-115.
Kanger, H. (1984), *Human Rights in the U.N. Declaration*, Almqvist and Wiksell International: Stockholm.
Lindahl, L. (1977), *Position and Change*, D. Reidel Publishing Company: Dordrecht.
Ost, D.E. (1984), 'The "Right" not to Know', *The Journal of Medicine and Philosophy*, Vol. 9, pp. 301-312.
Pörn, I. (1970), *The Logic of Power*, Basil Blackwell: Oxford.
Tapper, C.F.H. (1973), 'Powers and Secondary Rules of Change', in Simpson, A.W.B. (ed.), *Oxford Essays in Jurisprudence*, pp. 242-277, Clarendon Press: Oxford.

5 Rights to know and not to know: Is there a need for a genetic privacy law?

Tony McGleenan

The development of genetic testing and screening techniques which can unravel ever increasing amounts of information about an individual's genetic composition offers clear challenges for lawyers and legislators. The fact that potential conflicts about genetic information are described in terms of 'rights' to know or not to know indicates that the discussion of these issues has already been transported into a quasi-legal framework (Kielstein and Sass, 1992, p. 395). This essay examines a possible legal context for the so-called 'rights' to know and not to know. Increasingly, those given the task of preempting the potential difficulties posed by the genetic revelation of future health information focus on the concept of genetic privacy. This essay considers this notion of genetic privacy and attempts to elucidate what, if any, light such a concept can shed on this already perplexing issue. At least five key issues need to be addressed to determine whether there is a need for a genetic privacy law. First, as there is no particular consensus as to what the concept of privacy actually involves, indeed one writer has identified 13 different legal senses by which the term is understood, (Flaherty, 1989) this essay attempts to trace the legal pedigree of privacy. In so doing it is important to enter the caveat that the concept of privacy under consideration is that which has evolved in Anglo-American jurisprudence. While there is a strong European civil law tradition of privacy which places great weight on the need to protect the human dignity of the individual this is subtly different from the Anglo-American tradition which is based on the 'right of individuals to limit access by others to some part of their persons.' (Gostin, 1995, p. 454). Attempting to assess both of these diverging formulations of privacy would undoubtedly confuse an already nebulous issue. Secondly, the question of whether the modern legal formulations of the concept of privacy can be developed or adapted in such a way as to provide remedies for genetic information disputes must be addressed. Thirdly, privacy is often discussed as if it were a free standing ethical principle. However, privacy seems, in fact, to be more of a secondary principle which tends to serve broader utilitarian concerns. This essay examines the precise ethical basis of the concept of privacy. Fourthly, the question of the need for genetic privacy legislation can be further illuminated by a study of a model piece of legislation drafted by the Ethical, Legal and Social Implications (ELSI) sub group of the Human Genome Project. This draft legislation, entitled the Genetic Privacy Act, proposes a series of procedural safeguards which, it is argued, will prohibit unauthorised use of private genetic information. (Annas, Glantz and Roche, 1995, p. 360). The merits of such a strategy and the likelihood that such a measure will prevent the abuse of genetic information are examined in some detail. Fifthly and finally, a key issue in this discussion is to ascertain what exactly genetic privacy laws are designed to achieve. It would seem that, alongside some other subsidiary concerns, the major difficulty posed by the sudden accumulation of private genetic information is the possibility of genetic discrimination. Ultimately the viability and value of any genetic privacy law is to be measured against the likelihood that it will minimise any such discrimination. This must be weighed against the fact that there are strong arguments from the standpoint of social solidarity as to why such laws should not be enacted. This essay assesses whether, on balance, the introduction of a genetic privacy law is likely to minimise the type of genetic information conflicts captured in the debates on the right to know or not to know.

The developing concept of privacy

The lack of privacy law in British jurisprudence is an issue which has led to numerous calls for the introduction of legislation to curb the excesses of intrusive media. However, it is in the United States that the concept of privacy has matured into a central feature of the legal landscape. Given the expansion of the concept of privacy in the United States, it is notable that prior to 1889 privacy did not exist as a legal concept. The development of privacy jurisprudence can be traced directly to the wedding of the daughter of Samuel Warren, a prominent Boston lawyer, in 1889. At that time the American newspaper industry had been revolutionised by the methods of the first media moguls and as a consequence tabloid journalism was born. The Boston newspapers reported the Warren wedding in sensational style (Gormley, 1992, p. 1348). In response Warren, along with a colleague, Louis Brandeis, wrote an article for the *Harvard Law Review* entitled 'The Right to Privacy' (Brandeis and Warren, 1890, p. 193). It is this article which has formed the corner-stone of the modern jurisprudence of privacy. Prior to its publication there had been no coherent articulation of a concept of privacy. There had, of course, been English common laws with a similar basis but none of these provided a right of action for an invasion of privacy.

While on one level, the article by Warren and Brandeis was written as an attack on the excesses of the newspaper industry, this in itself cannot explain its lasting impact nor why it has had such an influence on the development of one of the most significant legal fields of the twentieth century. Rather, the enduring quality of the argument put by Warren and Brandeis lies in their careful sketching of the right to privacy. Drawing on a long and colourful list of English and Irish case law, they argued that there existed within the common law, a right to privacy which could be described quite simply as 'the right to be let alone'. Warren and Brandeis argued for the creation of a new tort which would provide individuals with a right of action on interference with their 'inviolate personality.'

Such a concept of privacy clearly has attractions for those wrestling with the difficulties posed by the potential for misuse of genetic information. After all, what could be more intrusive to the individual's 'inviolate personality' than an unauthorised disclosure of their genetic composition? Over a century after the seminal article was penned it is possible to look back at the development of privacy jurisprudence in the United States in an effort to discern whether the right to privacy contains the basis for a legal framework for resolving or preventing genetic information disputes. Being let alone has a strong intuitive appeal in the context of genetic testing and screening. Individuals may well wish to be 'let alone' and protected from receiving unwanted genetic information. Equally they may wish to be shielded from any compulsion or coercion to reveal genetic information which they regard as part of their 'inviolate personality'. This intuitive appeal can be explored further by examining the modern formulations of privacy to assess whether these could provide a legal basis for the protection of genetic information and a resolution of conflicts about the rights to know or not to know.

Genetic information and the modern laws of privacy

At least four distinct forms of privacy law have been developed in the United States. The first category could be described as the right to be let alone with respect to the acquisition and dissemination of personal information concerning the individual. This area of the law has developed in response to unauthorised publication, photography and other media intrusions. It encompasses the original tort of privacy as envisaged by Warren and Brandeis, and has been described as a law which is designed to give individuals a form of editorial control over how they establish their identities and how they are viewed by society (Gross, 1971, p. 175).

A second species of privacy law which may also be of relevance to the debate on genetic information is that of 4th Amendment privacy. This has been described as the right to be let alone with respect to government searches and seizures which invade the sphere of the individual. This form of privacy has always been an inherent part of the common law, but it has been developed to the extent that a right of privacy has been imported by interpretation into the Constitution itself. Thus it has been stated that the 4th Amendment:

> protects Americans in their beliefs, their thoughts, their emotions and their sensations. They [the framers] conferred as against the Government, the right to be let alone - the most comprehensive of rights and the right most valued by civilised men (1928, p. 478-479).

This area of privacy law is constantly expanding. In the modern environment an individual often has much more to worry about than the integrity of his or her castle. Might not the structure of an individual's genetic information stored on a computer database require equal protection from unjustifiable search and seizure, if not by governments, then by corporations and insurance companies?

The third genus of privacy jurisprudence can be described as the right to be let alone when one individual's freedom of speech threatens to disrupt another's liberty of thought and space. The case law in this area has developed around the concept of preserving the privacy of individuals by protecting them from information they do not wish to receive. This area of the law developed as a consequence of the unprecedented increase in the number of door to door brush salesmen in the United States in the depression of the 1930's. Cities and states passed legislation to prohibit 'solicitors, peddlers, hawkers, itinerant merchants and transient vendors' from going to private homes. This was challenged in *Breard v City of Alexandria* (1947) where Mr. Breard claimed he had the right to solicit subscriptions for home shopping catalogues. The US Supreme Court, however, upheld the right of the individual to be protected from unwanted information. This notion of protecting the individual from unsolicited information clearly has a strong resonance with the current debates on the right not to know genetic information. Perhaps a principle formulated to stop harassment from travelling salespeople could be developed in order to form the basis of a right not to be burdened with unwanted genetic information.

The fourth type of privacy law is known as fundamental decision privacy and provides that individuals have the right to be let alone in relation to fundamental personal decisions. The impact of this form of privacy law can be seen when we consider perhaps the most famous case to take place under this area of privacy, the landmark Supreme Court decision in *Roe v Wade* (1973). In that case the court ruled that the right of privacy, implicitly contained in the 14th amendment of the Constitution:

> was broad enough to encompass a woman's decision whether or not to terminate her pregnancy

The decision in *Roe v Wade* and the development of this type of privacy law has to a large extent been technologically led. Medical advances have created a sphere of personal choice which could not have been envisaged when Warren and Brandeis developed the law of privacy in 1890. The invention of new types of medical techniques have made abortion a relatively safe and widely available procedure, but have also allowed individuals to make fundamental personal decisions in an area where the state often claims an interest. Privacy in this context has developed as a right of autonomy or a right to be left alone while making fundamental life decisions. Genetic technology and genetic screening open up an ever greater vista for personal choice. Individuals screened for genetic diseases will be faced with fundamental personal decisions in which others will have an interest, not just the state but relatives, employers and insurers. In some cases these interests will be legitimate and perhaps privacy rights ought to be balanced against other considerations. In other cases the interest may be more sinister, for example an insurance company which hacks into a computer database in order to obtain medical records. Against such possibilities protection of privacy seems essential and the principles contained in the fundamental decision privacy might well repay careful consideration.

The ethical basis of privacy

The discussion of the genesis and development of the concept of privacy illustrates the position of primacy it has achieved at least in the legal system of the United States. It would not be unreasonable to assume that a legal principle which has acquired such significance must be based on extremely solid ethical foundations. The considerable literature which has developed around the jurisprudence of privacy typically contains involved and detailed descriptions of what the concept of privacy actually means along complex formulae setting out the situations in which it can be applied. It is altogether more difficult to find a comprehensive analysis of the ethical basis of privacy. This is somewhat surprising in that privacy is often argued for on the basis that it is a legal 'trump', an overriding principle which should transcend other values. If privacy is such a principle then one would expect some degree of consensus as to the ethical basis of such a principle, indeed it could only be justified as an overarching and all conquering legal principle if it were based on extremely strong ethical foundations.

However, privacy does not have any such ethical basis. Undoubtedly there are strong moral arguments for the protection of the privacy of individuals. Respecting the privacy of individuals is desirable insofar as it respects or enhances the autonomy of individuals. Gostin argues that privacy is an important means of fostering and developing a strong sense of personhood, and that it facilitates the development and maintenance of personal and professional relationships (Gostin, 1995, p. 514). These arguments themselves suggest that privacy is a derivative concept which is constructed to serve broader, generally, utilitarian concerns. As such it is possible to override the demands of privacy when more compelling arguments can be made for disclosure of information which serve the same utilitarian goals. It is undeniable that such trade-offs are regularly made in modern health care. The collection of large quantities of medical information on computer database is widely tolerated, even in the United States, because such practices ultimately facilitate the development and operation of an efficient health information system, without which modern health care systems cannot function. Inevitably, breaches of individual privacy will occur in the operation of such systems, but the moral claims of privacy can be subjugated to other stronger societal claims. As Gostin points out:

> Individuals already forego significant levels of privacy in order to obtain the social goods that benefit society collectively. Many of the collective goals of society, ranging from law enforcement and public safety to tax collection and national security are achieved partly by collection of personal information ... A complex modern society cannot elevate each person's interest in privacy above other important societal interests.

Privacy often does conflict with other interests and given that it does not have the type of ethical foundation which would permit it to act as a legal principle which can 'trump' all others then it is inevitable that in some circumstances privacy claims will be compromised. It is arguable that the strongest conflicts with privacy interests will arise in areas where collective social solidarity is suggested. This is particularly significant in relation to genetic information since it is possible that the best means of minimising the harmful potential of genetic screening and testing is to take legislative and other measures which have as their objective the strengthening of a sense of social solidarity. In so far as privacy concepts place the rights of the individual above the interests of society they may ultimately serve to aggravate rather than ameliorate the problems posed by genetic information.

The ELSI Genetic Privacy Act

Under the Human Genome Project a significant proportion of the funding has been channelled into research into the ethical, legal and social implications of genetic technology. This work which takes place under the umbrella of the ELSI group has led a team of researchers, led by George Annas, to develop a Genetic Privacy Act (Annas, Glantz and Roche, 1995). In their commentary to the draft legislation the authors outline the objectives of the proposed legislation:

> the overarching premise of the Act is that no stranger should have or control identifiable DNA samples or genetic information about an

individual unless that individual specifically authorises the collection of DNA samples for the purpose of genetic analysis, authorises the creation of genetic information, and has access to, and control over the dissemination of that information.

The legislation is structured in terms of researcher/clinician obligations and patient or sample source rights. Under the Act any person who screens an individual or who collects a DNA sample must verbally provide specific information prior to collection of the DNA sample.[1] Secondly, he or she must provide the patient with a notice of rights and assurances prior to the collection of the DNA sample.[2] Thirdly, there is an obligation to obtain written authorisation for the screening or testing [3] and to restrict access to the samples to those persons who are authorised by the screened or tested person.[4] Finally, the person collecting the DNA must abide by the sample source's instruction in relation to the maintenance[5] and destruction of DNA samples.[6]

In addition to the obligations placed on the clinician the sample source has certain rights explicitly set out in the Act. Thus he or she can determine who may collect and analyse DNA. The sample source can determine the purposes for which a sample can be analysed and have the right to know what information can reasonably be expected to be derived from the analysis. The sample source has the right to order its destruction and to delegate this authority to a third party after death.[7] The source also has the right to refuse permission for the sample to be used for commercial or research activities and to obtain copies of any records which emerge from the analysis (Genetic Privacy Act, 1995, s. 103:8).

However, the legislation contains a large number of exceptions to the overarching principle of privacy set out by the drafters. Genetic information can be disclosed for use in a law enforcement proceeding in which the person holding the information is the subject of the proceedings.[8] In addition, disclosure of genetic material is permissible where it is needed for identification in law enforcement proceedings. The Act also contains provision for the issuance of a court order to compel the disclosure of private genetic information where:

(1) other ways of obtaining the private genetic information are not available or would not be effective ; and
(2) there is a compelling need for the private genetic information which outweighs the potential harm to the privacy interest of the subject of the information (Genetic Privacy Act, 1995, s.115(d)).

Genetic information may also be used for research purposes provided that a research ethics committee has given its approval.[9] The issue of the right to know is explicitly considered in s. 133 of the Act which states that where:

a relative of a deceased sample source is at risk of a genetic disease which in reasonable medical judgment could be effectively ameliorated, prevented or treated, nothing in this Act shall be construed as prohibiting researchers from contacting such relatives and informing them of the risk.

The legislation also permits the taking of samples from children (Genetic Privacy Act, 1995, ss. 141-142) and incompetent persons (Genetic Privacy Act, 1995, s. 143). In the case of incompetent persons the analysis must be necessary to diagnose the cause of incompetence and any information so obtained can be disclosed where necessary for the diagnosis of a proven genetic condition (Genetic Privacy Act, 1995, s. 144).

Is there a need for a genetic privacy law?

The Genetic Privacy Act is a thorough and well constructed piece of draft legislation. However, the Act may lean too heavily in favour of disclosure of genetic information. This in itself is not a fatal flaw. A liberal approach to disclosure of private genetic information only becomes a problem if we accept the maintenance of confidentiality of genetic medical records as a paramount social goal. If we do not accept this as a foundational ethical principle then the compromises and trade-offs which characterise the Genetic Privacy Act will seem entirely acceptable if not eminently sensible. However, it can be argued that the value of such legislation should not be assessed according to how much or how little access to genetic information is permitted. Access to genetic information is not a problem in itself, each of us carries a great deal of totally accessible genetic information in our personal appearance. This information is freely available to the world at large, it only becomes a problem when that 'information', whether skin colour of facial characteristic is used to deny the individual rights or privileges which would have been available had those characteristics not been known. Ultimately the root of the problem does not lie in the accessibility or otherwise of genetic information, but arises because of the discriminatory and prejudicial attitudes within society. The key question in assessing the validity of, and, indeed the need for any genetic privacy legislation, is whether the envisaged legislation will address these problems of genetic discrimination. If the proposed legislation does not directly address the problems of discrimination and is not drafted with this as a paramount consideration then it is arguable that any such law is just as likely to exacerbate the problem. The experience of HIV testing suggests that the major difficulties arise because of the significant misunderstandings which occur in relation to the outcomes of testing and also because of the high risk of discrimination (Parmet, 1995, p. 372). The legislative response to HIV testing in many jurisdictions has largely been the implementation of procedural restrictions on the collection and dissemination of information. However, these restrictions have not been entirely successful in preventing discriminatory practices by employers and insurance companies against those who are HIV positive (*McGann v. H. & H Music*

Company, p. 403). Indeed, Parmet suggests that the ineffectuality of the procedural approach is demonstrated by the fact that between 25 percent and 30 percent of HIV positive individuals in the United States have no health insurance cover (Bartrum, 1993, p. 251). Drawing on this experience Parmet argues that procedurally based genetic privacy laws will be similarly ineffective:

> As with HIV statutes, if procedures are followed, disclosures about genetic information can still occur. Insurers will still be able to discriminate. Information can still be widely disbursed ... If the experience with HIV offers any lessons it is that until the reasons for collecting genetic information are more fully agreed on, the privacy ensured may be more illusory than real (Parmet, 1995).

The Genetic Privacy Act drafted by the ELSI initiative provides a valuable case study against which we can test this analysis. The premise of the Act and the objectives of those who drafted it have already been stated above, and it is notable that the issue of genetic discrimination is not explicitly addressed. The difficulty with procedural legislation of the type proposed by the ELSI programme is that powerful interest groups such as insurance companies and major employers have a wealth of experience in circumventing the strictures of procedural legislation. A piece of legislation which is as riddled with exceptions as the Genetic Privacy Act will pose no particular difficulties to those determined to ascertain private genetic information about the individual. In addition, the introduction of procedural safeguards promotes a sense of individualism and insecurity in which the individual citizen, or sample source to use the dehumanising moniker, is encouraged in the belief that private genetic information is a potentially harmful substance which is best kept as secret as possible, even to the extent that the information should be withheld from close relatives who may derive a direct benefit from the sharing of the information (Suter, 1993, p. 1877). The development of a mindset which suggests that genetic information is dangerous is one which is likely to cause as much harm as the creation of a DNA database for research purposes.

Rather than focusing on the development of privacy laws and procedural safeguards which ring-fence the use of genetic information legislators should focus their attention on minimising the threatening potential of genetic information. Currently, the major threat to the individual from genetic information is that it may be used to deny opportunities and facilities which are regarded as essential in a modern society. Unscrupulous use of private genetic information could lead to the denial of employment, of mortgages, pensions, loans and of life and health insurance. Undoubtedly, genetic privacy laws could prove to be a useful tool in minimising the impact of such discriminatory conduct but they can only ever be partially successful. The introduction of privacy laws may just as readily contribute to the erosion of a sense of social solidarity which is arguably the best available protection against the fragmentation of modern societies which may well occur if the worst excesses of genetic determinism materialise (Miller, 1989, p. 733). A more appropriate legislative response to the difficulties posed by the uncovering of large quantities of predictive genetic information is to foster a climate where there is no particular need to conceal this information, because no detrimental consequences will flow from its revelation. This might best be achieved by the introduction of laws which are targeted at the use and misuse of genetic information rather than the collection and storage of it.

Notes

1   s. 101(b) 'Prior to the collection of a DNA sample from a sample source for genetic analysis, the person collecting the sample or causing the sample to be collected shall verbally inform the sample source or the sample sources' representative.'

2   s. 105 'A person who collects or stores DNA samples for genetic analysis shall provide a sample source or a sample source's representative prior to the collection, storage or analysis of a DNA sample, and any other person upon request, with a notice of rights and assurances'

3   s. 101(a) 'no person may collect or cause to be collected an individually identifiable DNA sample for genetic analysis without the written authorisation of the sample source or the sample source's representative'

4   s. 112 This section establishes a series of requirements to be met before an authorisation for disclosure of private genetic information will be considered valid.

5   s. 102 'genetic analysis of an individually identifiable DNA sample is prohibited unless specifically authorised in writing by the sample source or the sample sources' relative'

6   s. 104 (c) 'An individually identifiable DNA sample must be destroyed on completion of genetic analysis unless:
(1) the sample source or the sample source's representative, has directed otherwise in writing, or
(2) all individual identifiers linking the sample to the sample source are destroyed.'

7   s. 104 (b) 'the sample source or the sample source's representative shall have the right to order the destruction of the DNA sample'

8   s. 115 (a) 'No person who maintains private genetic information may be compelled to disclose such information pursuant to a request for compulsory disclosure in any judicial, legislative or administrative proceeding, unless: ...
(3) The genetic information is for use in a law enforcement proceeding or investigation in which the person maintaining the information is the subject or party.'

9   s. 132 (a) 'Any person who, in the ordinary course of business, practice of a profession, or rendering of a service, stores or maintains private genetic

information is prohibited from allowing access to such information to researchers unless:

(1) an Institutional Review Board has approved the conduct of the research program or study; and;

(2) the sample source or the sample source's representative has specifically consented to the access or disclosure of such information in an authorisation that meets the requirements of s. 112.

References

Annas, G.J., Glantz, L.H. and Roche, P.A. (1995), 'Drafting the Genetic Privacy Act: Science, Policy and Practical Considerations', *Journal of Law, Medicine and Ethics*, Vol. 23, pp. 360-366.

Annas, G.J., Glantz, L.H. and Roche, P.A. (1995), *The Genetic Privacy Act and Commentary*, Boston University School of Public Health. Available at http://www-bushph.bu.edu/Depts/HealthLaw/

Bartrum, T.E. (1993), 'Fear, Discrimination and Dying in the Workplace: AIDS and the Capping of Employee Health Insurance Benefits', *Kentucky Law Journal*, Vol. 82, pp. 249-284.

Billings, P. and Beckwith, J. (1992) 'Genetic Testing in the Workplace: A View from the USA', *Trends in Genetics*, Vol. 8, p. 198-202.

Brandeis, L. and Warren, S. (1890), 'The Right to Privacy', *Harvard Law Review*, Vol. 4, pp. 193-221.

Breard v City of Alexandria 46 F 2d 337 (1947, DC La).

Flaherty, D. (1989), *Protecting Privacy in Surveillance Societies*, University of North Carolina Press.

Gormley, K. (1992) 'One Hundred Years of Privacy', *Wisconsin Law Review*, pp. 1335-1441.

Gostin, L. (1991) 'Genetic Discrimination: The Use of Genetically Based Diagnostic and Prognostic Tests by Employers and Insurers', *American Journal of Law & Medicine*, Vol. 17, p. 109-144.

Gostin, L. (1995), 'Health Information Privacy', *Cornell Law Review*, Vol. 80, pp. 451-527.

Gross, H. (1971) 'Privacy and Autonomy' in Pennock, J.R. and Chapman, J.W. (eds) , *Privacy*, pp.169-91, New York Atherton Press: New York.

Kielstein, R. and Sass, H. (1992), 'Right not to Know or Duty to Know? Prenatal Screening for Polycystic Renal Disease', *Journal of Medicine and Philosophy*, Vol. 17, pp. 395-405.

McGann v H & H Music Co. 946 F.2d at 403.

Miller, J.M. (1989), 'Genetic Testing and Insurance Classification: National Action Can Prevent Discrimination based on the 'Luck of the Genetic Draw', *Dickinson Law Review*, Vol. 93, pp. 729-757.

*Olmstead v United States.*277 U.S.at 478-479 (1928).

Parmet, W.E. (1995), 'Legislating Privacy: The HIV Experience', *Journal of Law, Medicine and Ethics*, Vol. 23, p. 371-376.

Roe v Wade U.S.113 (1973).

Rothstein, M.A. (1993), 'Discrimination Based on Genetic Information', *Jurimetrics Journal*, Vol. 33, p. 13-18.

Suter, S.M. (1993), 'Whose Genes Are These Anyway? Familial Conflict over Access to Genetic Information', *Michigan Law Review*, Vol. 91, pp. 1854-1908.

6 Autonomy and a right not to Know

Jørgen Husted

A problem out of a problem

Genetics and diseases of genetic origin inescapably involve families. Thus genetic information obtained by testing one person may contain information of the same kind on one or more other persons. These other persons are so to speak being tested indirectly by the original test. Now, the justification for testing the first person is the recognition that this person has an interest in knowing the relevant information. The knowledge may be sought to gain a better background for reproductive decisions or for undertaking measures preventive of future health problems caused by genetic disease or susceptibility. This leads to the conclusion that each of the other persons concerned has the same interest in knowing the information on herself or himself.

But suppose the person who has undergone the test does not want the findings to be passed on to the other family members? In its report on the ethical issues of genetic screening the Nuffield Council on Bioethics offers the following example:

> A man diagnosed with a mild form of adrenoleukodystrophy (ALD), an X-linked condition that can be carried by healthy females, did not wish his diagnosis or the genetic implications to be discussed with his family. Seven years later, his niece gave birth to two successive boys who have a more severe form of ALD. The illness only came to light in them when the elder boy started to display symptoms. The mother's sister, the man's other niece, has also given birth to a son subsequently diagnosed with ALD. Both families are bitterly resentful that the medical services did not

55

warn them of their genetic risk. (Nuffield Council on Bioethics, 1993, p. 42)

In this kind of situation an ethical dilemma arises between the right of the individual to personal privacy on the one hand and the interest of family members to be made fully aware of available information which would play a part in making important life decisions on the other. More directly it presents itself to the doctor as a conflict between the duty of confidentiality owed to the patient and the regard for the third parties who are likely to be harmed or at least forego a major benefit due to nondisclosure. The doctor's duty of confidentiality is strongly supported by two considerations, the individual's right to privacy and the upholding of trust and confidence in the doctor/patient relationship generally. However, as the Nuffield Report (1993) and also Ruth Macklin (1992) point out, this duty is not absolute. In very special circumstances it may be overruled in the public interest or for preventing injury or severe health damage to other individuals. Both argue that the same kind of exceptional overruling may apply to the genetic context as well. No general rule can be given and the doctor has to perform a very delicate exercise in balancing the risks and harms of nondisclosure against those of disclosure. Ruth Macklin suggests that there are cases, albeit few, in which an actual duty to disclose genetic information emerges (1992, p. 163). The Nuffield Report concludes that the third party's interest is to be considered strong enough to support 'a legitimate right to know' and it even discusses, though finally rejecting it primarily out of pragmatic reasons, whether there should be a legally enforceable duty of disclosure to family members placed on people who have been tested and on their medical service (Nuffield Council on Bioethics, 1993, p. 53).

Now, in this ethical problem another one seems to be lurking in the background. If the person who has been tested or that person's doctor, perhaps overruling the duty of confidentiality, approaches the unsuspecting family member with the findings this latter person is quite defenceless. As it seems, the alleged right to know does not comprise a right not to know. By the very approach the 'cat has been let out of the bag'. Either this person comes to know the new personal information or, at least, comes know that there is something to know that is considered quite urgent for her or him to know. A wholly new situation has been created - the irreversible loss of genetic informational innocence is a *fait accompli*.

Paternalism revived?

A first reaction to this problem could be to acknowledge that there is a significant difference in status between the two persons involved. Whereas the first person has given informed consent both to being tested and to being informed of the findings the latter person definitely has not. However, the requirement of obtaining informed consent is meant to ensure voluntariness and adequate understanding - that is, to rule out any form of compulsion, deceit, misinformation and manipulation - as a necessary condition for performing a medical intervention on a person. This requirement clearly applied to the first person, this being a case of a person who has to decide whether to undergo a medical intervention or not. In the case of the unwitting family member there is no medical intervention and the relative or the doctor is only offering to impart some already available information that the person has a clear interest in knowing.

If one is to take the principle of informed consent seriously this reaction will not do. The principle grew out of the critique of medical paternalism according to which the doctor is justified to act, with or without consent, to promote what is perceived from the medical point of view as the patient's best interest. As the doctor is taken to be in a position best to know what is best for the individual patient the so-called therapeutical privilege gives the doctor the right of usurping the decision making, even in relation to fully competent adult persons. One major point urged against medical paternalism was the simple one that since a person can have different and competing interests what is all in all in this person's best interest might very well be different from what is perceived as such from the narrow medical point of view. In itself this point strongly supports the requirement of informed consent. Now, the justification for performing the genetic test on the first family member was not that this person has an interest in knowing the relevant information (the interest shared with the family member). The justification was that this person after mature and well-informed consideration decided to give priority to this interest of her or his. However, the very fact that the other family member has the same interest in no way at all justifies the assumption that she or he would reach the same decision. Thus the unsolicited disclosure, whether by the relative following the doctor's strong suggestion or by the doctor acting independently, seems to be a clear cut case of strong medical paternalism - acting solely from the medical point of view the decision 'To know or not to know?' is taken out of the hands of the unsuspecting individual, for her or his own good of course.

A more sophisticated response grants the above but seeks to put the matter in the right light by linking informed consent directly to the concept of (personal) autonomy. According to this the very point of insisting on the principle of informed consent in the medical context is to uphold in this area too a general right to autonomy, that is, a right for persons to make important decisions defining their own lives for themselves. What is wrong about medical paternalism is not so much the assumption that the doctor knows best as the usurpation of decision making. Ethics demands fundamentally that adult persons of normal competence be respected as responsible decision makers in matters pertaining to themselves. The important thing is not that the best decision is found, but that the person concerned reaches a decision that she or he considers the best. Denying people this right to autonomy, even out of the most benevolent motives, is denying them respect for their dignity as persons, as beings who are able to think and choose for themselves. Now in the case of unsolicited disclosure the decision to know or not to know is of course being taken out of the hands of the person concerned. This case is, however, significantly different form the much criticised cases of paternalism where the doctor decides on irreversible interventions without consulting the patient about her or his view on the alternatives. This constitutes a clear reduction of autonomy, a closing of options, and is being done in the name of other values than autonomy, e.g. welfare, health or survival. In the case of unsolicited disclosure, on the other hand, what initially seems to be a denial of autonomy is just the opposite - it is done in the name of autonomy and the result is an enhancement of autonomy, an opening of options. As the important information has become available and now is there to be made use of or not, is it not quite clear that a respect for persons as decision makers demands that they be given and not denied this information? Maybe some persons will resent the disclosure, at least as a first reaction, and will come to worry and agonise about new challenges and fears. But all this is part and parcel of being a responsible decision maker. Thus the challenge of paternalism can be evaded. Unsolicited disclosure violates autonomy in a formal sense, but respects and enhances it in a substantial sense - the very one that makes the formal one so important. In her discussion of a duty to disclose Ruth Macklin puts this way of thinking quite clearly:

> If such information (viz. genetic information that can substantially affect a patient's relatives) is disclosed, it can enable them to make reproductive decisions and other life plans in accordance with the newly revealed information. Without adequate information, people cannot make informed choices and decisions related to their own health and well-being (Macklin, 1992, p. 163).

In this way unsolicited disclosure to relatives seems quite unproblematic from an ethical point of view.

The Nuffield Report dwells on several psychological problems, especially arising where some family members do not wish to be presented with the information, and notes ' ... that this would become a much more serious problem if widespread screening were introduced for X-linked or autosomal dominant diseases.' (Nuffield Council on Bioethics, 1993, p. 49)

In view of this latter remark and the astonishing speed of the development of genetic research it is important to investigate further the above reasoning that tends to give unsolicited disclosure to unwitting relatives a firmly established and ethically unproblematic place in clinical practice. Since the concept of autonomy is pivotal in the justifying reasoning this is where to proceed.

Autonomy: the thin conception

Although there is only one concept of autonomy there are, when it comes to explaining it, several conceptions of autonomy. For the purpose at hand the following two will suffice. Both agree that autonomy is the running of one's own life according to one's own lights: people are said to be autonomous to the extent to which they are able to fashion their own lives, and to some extent their own destiny, by the exercise of their own faculties in successive choices during their lives. The first - thin - conception of autonomy aims to explain the autonomous person and the autonomous life by way of explaining the kind of choice characteristically made by the former and defining the latter, *viz* the autonomous individual choice. The idea is that an agent's decision will be maximally autonomous where:

1 there are no apparent defects in the individual's ability to control either his or her desires or actions or both;

2 there are no apparent defects in reasoning, or no defects in reasoning which would bear on the validity of the conclusions upon which the agent's decisions are based;

3 there are no apparent defects in the information available to the agent and which are germane to the decision at hand (Harris, 1985, p. 201).

The usual background for this thin account of autonomy is a preference or desire satisfaction theory of the good for persons. According to this, what is good for persons is for them to have their desires or preferences satisfied to the maximum extent possible over their lifetimes. So on the one hand there is the person's wishes or preferences. Some of these are short-term ones, others are long-term wishes, perhaps even a life plan. Among the latter could be wishes for the following: a happy family life, good health, beauty, wealth, power, social prestige, deep involvements with other people, personal independence, self-realisation, to see the world, leading a quiet and pleasant life, enjoying oneself as much as possible, strong and varied excitements, intellectual achievement, a successful career in a certain walk of life, social and spiritual security etc. Given his or her long-term preferences the person successively develops short-term preferences whose satisfaction is considered conducive of the long-term ones, e.g. having at least three healthy children, taking up a career in dentistry, keeping fit, travelling etc. The person's wishes or preferences is something given about him or her: the person so to speak finds himself or herself as a person with this kind of inclination. They are the person's own wishes, part of the individual's set-up. Also, they can only be criticised rationally in so far as they can be shown to be either clearly unrealistic or based on false beliefs. On the other hand there is the person's decisions and actions. Their whole point is the instrumental one of contributing to the person's good by serving the satisfaction of his or her short-term and long-term preferences. Thus they can be criticised rationally as more or less well-informed, well considered, realistic or well suited to achieve various goals. An important consideration here is of course whether they are autonomous in the above sense.

This approach offers a very clear justification of the principle of informed consent in health care, at least as soon as it is recognised that the goal is the promotion of the individual's good, not just his or her health. Thus R.M. Hare:

> ... on the whole people are the best judges of what will be best for them in the future. They are likely to predict more correctly than any doctor what will best for *themselves*. For people's ideas of what is a good life vary enormously, and doctors are, these days, seldom in a position to know a patient well enough to predict them. The doctor can usually predict better than the patient what the consequences of a particular treatment will be; but he is not expert on how the patient will like these consequences. Therefore, in deciding on a treatment, the doctor should be guided by the patient's idea of the best life, and not impose his own (Hare, 1994, p. 154).

Since people generally are the best judges of their own good their autonomous decisions relating to that matter should be respected. A doctor is always in the wrong if he or she goes against a person's autonomous decision of this kind. First, the doctor actually wrongs this person by acting against the person's good and, second, the doctor jeopardises the whole relationship between doctors and the public as much harm is likely to ensue both for the profession as a whole and for individual patients, if autonomy comes to be disregarded.

Now, seen from this ethical perspective the above, preliminary characterisation of unsolicited disclosure as ethically quite unproblematic can be endorsed. First of all, in such cases there is clearly no question of doing the wrong thing, *viz* going against a person's autonomous decision relating to his or her own good. Also, the information revealed is information of great importance for the individual's ability to make decisions and consider short-term preferences with a view to achieving the maximal satisfaction of long-term preferences. Thus, revealing the information is, very literally, for the person's own good.

Though everything now seems well and good there remains a problem and this points toward the second - thick - conception of autonomy. A person may decide to undergo a genetic test the result of which is very likely to devastate his or her life by revealing an incurable condition that will mean the end within a few years of him or her and all his or her aspirations for himself or herself. His or her reason for doing this is to provide vital information for a number of his or her close relatives. As he or she is the first to admit, it is definitely not done for his or her own good in the above sense. Quite on the contrary, the person decides against his or her own good, sacrificing it out of a deeply felt moral obligation overruling all of his or her personal preferences. The problem, now, is that according to the principle of informed consent his/her decision should be respected even though it, by his or her own admission, is not an autonomous decision of the kind that was crucially appealed to in the above justification for this principle, *viz* an autonomous decision in the area where the person concerned is the best judge - pertaining to promoting his or her own good. Going against a person's decision of that kind would be wrong although it would not be an instance of the wrong thing just explained, *viz* going against a person's autonomous choice relating to his or her own good. There are many well-known cases of this kind - e.g. people who decide to forego necessary medical treatment either because they believe other people need it more or because they want the expenses avoided in order to save the money for the benefit of e.g. a daughter's education. What they show is that the justification of the principle of informed consent is not fully explained by reference to the claim that people are the best judges of their own good. This claim has to be supplemented by independent considerations.[1]

Autonomy: the thick conception

In the following quotation the gist of this way of thinking is eloquently expressed by Sir Isaiah Berlin:

> I wish my life and decision to depend on myself, not on external forces of whatever kind. I wish to be the instrument of my own, not of other men's acts of will. I wish to be a subject, not an object; to be moved by reasons, by conscious purposes, which are my own, not by causes which affect me, as it were, from outside. I wish to be somebody, not anybody; a doer - deciding not being decided for, self-directed and not acted upon by external nature or by other men ... I wish, above all, to be conscious of myself as a thinking, willing, active being, bearing responsibility for his choices and able to explain them by reference to his own ideas and purposes (Berlin, 1969, p. 123).

The ideal of the person outlined here is the ideal of personal autonomy as self-determination, or self-definition.[2] It is readily contrasted with the preference satisfaction theory of the good for persons. First, a person's decisions and actions are not seen as of primarily an instrumental function and value, as the means for achieving the satisfaction of already given preferences. Instead human well-being is thought of under the category of activity, as the successful pursuit of freely chosen goals, the thought being that what persons are is, in significant respects, what they become through successive choices and actions during their lives - that their lives are a continuous process of self-creation. What makes a life *ours* is that is fashioned by our choices, is selected from alternatives by a human being taking his or her life seriously and wanting to be, and be recognised as by others as, the kind of person who makes decisions and accepts the responsibility for them.

Also, a person's preferences or goals are not to be considered as given and outside the reach of critical evaluation. What makes self-determination possible is the unique capacity of the human person for reflective self-evaluation, for considering what they want their motivations to be, for forming higher-order wants and preferences defining what they for themselves find it *worth being* and *worth doing* in life and trying, sometimes successfully sometimes not, to change their given preferences and inclinations in light of what they have come to care about, their higher-order goals and values. By exercising this capacity persons determine their lives and themselves, create meaning and coherence and take responsibility for their lives and character.

It is here of great importance to distinguish between autonomy as an achievement, the autonomous life created by the person, and autonomy as a capacity. To lead an autonomous life a person needs to have certain conditions fulfilled during this life. These are the various mental and linguistic abilities needed to exercise self-evaluation and self-control, independence in the sense of absence of external interference with decision processes and with actions, and a reasonable range of valuable options in the important self-defining situations throughout the various periods of life. Personal autonomy in the primary sense is the first one here, the idea of an autonomous life. Also what primarily has value is the autonomous life, the value of autonomy in the capacity sense being only contributional to this, not of value independently of its use. Autonomous decisions are, ideally, decisions that fit into an autonomous life, a life freely chosen. And as Joseph Raz puts it:

> It is a life which is here primarily judged as autonomous or not, and it is so judged by its history ... the autonomous life is discerned not by what there is in it but by how it came to be. It is discerned, if you like, by what it might have been and by why it is not other than it is (Raz, 1986, p. 371)

In this connection Raz argues very convincingly that autonomy and the kind of autonomous choosing that is constitutive of self-determination requires not only a free choice but a choice between valuable or good options. In a sense the choice between good and evil is no choice at all. Someone with the choice between becoming an electrician and having to murder someone else is not choosing autonomously if he or she chooses to become an electrician. His or her choice is forced: if he or she wants to be moral, he or she has no choice, being forced to fight for 'moral survival':

> Autonomy requires a choice of goods. A choice between good and evil is not good enough. Remember that it is personal, not moral autonomy we are concerned with. No doubt is cast on the fact that the person in the example is a moral and fully responsible person. So are the inmates of

concentration camps. But they do not have personal autonomy (Raz, 1986, p. 379).

Now the general point of the right to autonomy can be explained in a new and, it seems, more satisfactory way. Respecting an individual right to autonomy is an important part of making self-creation possible. The point of the right is to protect and encourage the capacity to take responsibility for one's life and express one's personality, commitments, convictions and vision of the good in the life one leads. And when people insist on their right to autonomy this is often done in the name of self-determination. They value being able to decide for themselves because they value being, and being recognised by others as, the kind of person who is capable of determining and taking responsibility for his or her destiny. To them the ideal of self-determination offers an attractive vision of what human beings can be and they hold this ideal for noninstrumental reasons - being recognised as a person capable of choosing and taking responsibility for her or his choices, and of course actually making choices of this kind has intrinsic value quite apart from the consequences and satisfactions flowing from it.

The principle of informed consent can now be seen as an application to the medical context of the right to autonomy explained in this way (Brock, 1993, chap. 1). What is wrong about medical paternalism is not primarily or solely that the doctor by deciding for the patient may be wrong, or more likely to be wrong than the patient himself or herself, in the estimation of the patient's good. What is wrong is the usurpation of decision making as such. Many of the decisions to be made in clinical practice, e.g. between alternative form of treatments or between treatment and nontreatment, are neither simple technical decisions nor are they decisions of the relatively simple kind where the task is to find the best solution given one or more rather clear personal preferences. Often the very idea of determining what is best is quite out of place. There is no question of who is the better judge of the patient's good, the doctor or the patient. A decision is called for, to choose this future or this other very different kind of future, to take responsibility for following this path ahead rather than another. Here the patient has to choose among values and the doctor's role is to help clarify the values, possibilities and consequences and, so far as possible, create valuable options suited to the individual's unique situation. In other words, many of the decisions to be made in clinical practice clearly belong to the self-defining kind of decisions that the right to autonomy is meant to protect and encourage.

From this new perspective the matter of the unsolicited disclosure of genetic findings to unsuspecting relatives begins to present itself as quite problematic. Taking the decision of whether to know or not to know out of the person's hands is a case of doing the wrong thing, being a clear case of usurpation of decision making. Also, the response that this violation of formal autonomy is justified by the enhancement of autonomy in a substantial sense is no good anymore. The fact that the person receives new and relevant information does not in itself justify a claim of enhancement of autonomy. Before turning more directly to the latter point it is worth noting that if the response were uncontroversial it would be quite difficult to make sense of the existing ethical codes for genetic testing stipulating the requirements of genetic counselling prior to testing, informed consent and non-directiveness in genetic counselling. The point of these requirements cannot just be to ensure voluntariness (no compulsion, manipulation etc.) and a proper level of information. Their point must be to make choice possible, it being recognised both that the choice to undergo a genetic test may have serious consequences of a kind that may make it fully understandable for a responsible and rational person to end up declining the offer of genetic testing. If the response appealing to the alleged enhancement of autonomy in the case of unsuspecting relatives were uncontroversial it would by the same token be quite uncontroversial for the doctor just to seek *assent* and not *informed consent* from the person invited to undergo a genetic test.

A mixed blessing?

As already mentioned, in their discussion of the dilemma between the doctor's duty of confidentiality and the relative's interest in knowing, need to know, or even the right to know both the Nuffield Report and Ruth Macklin cite cases to show that the duty of confidentiality is not absolute. The relevant cases stem from outside the field of applied human genetics, dealing with very dangerous mentally ill patients or patients with dangerous infectious diseases. Here the third party needs to be warned that somebody is out to kill or grievously harm her or him in one way or the other. In the genetic context the kind of information to be received by the unwitting relative is of course of a totally different character. Here a person may learn things of the following kind about himself or herself:

1   that the person is a carrier so that having children by another carrier might result in children with serious health problems.

2   that the person is a carrier who risks having children with serious health problems and/or passing this very unwanted condition on to future generations.

3   that the person has a disease likely to be passed on to the eventual offspring and future generations.

4   that the person has a presymptomatic condition that is likely to develop into a condition with serious symptoms unless the person undertakes certain draconian measures (radical change of lifestyle, frequent medical check ups, preventive surgery etc.).

5   that the person has a genetic predisposition that may develop into serious disease unless precautions are taken - and maybe anyhow.

6   that the person has a genetic susceptibility for a serious multifactorial disease that may be triggered by various environmental, psychological and other more or less unknown factors that the persons should have to guard himself or herself against.

7   that the person suffers from a genetic disease, the manifest outbreak of which may be postponed and made less severe if the person changes his or her life in various drastic ways.

Now, in stark contrast to the cases involving warning about highly dangerous persons and infectious diseases information of this kind is likely to have a great impact not only on people's feelings but on their lives as a whole. Reactions like the following ones are obviously to be expected:

1   a decision not to marry and thus not to seek deep emotional involvement with members of the opposite sex.

2   a married couple's decision not to have children of their own.

3   trying to avoid any kind of dependants and deep involvement with other people.

4   a married couple's decision not to have any further children.

5   terminating one's one and only pregnancy by selective abortion.

6   giving up a career one has built the major part of one's life around.

7   not to marry the person with whom one is deeply in love and to try to find a genetically more suitable partner for life and family making.

8   resigning in choosing a very attractive career or education for which one clearly has the ability.

9   giving up most of the things in one's life that one enjoys and finds worth doing.

10   trying to avoid all kind of life challenges that are bound to tax one's resources and, if one is to succeed, put one under great and long-term strain.

Of course, there are alternatives to all such decisions of paramount importance to the individual's self-definition. The person can always choose to ignore the benevolent genetic warnings and just go ahead with the life she or he has embarked, or is embarking, on. The person may marry, may marry the beloved one, have the children God gives, pursue the career and life style of his or her choice with full vigour, become deeply entwined in other people's lives, accepting all the worthy challenges that life throws in the way, hoping, dreaming, planning and striving for the kind of life-allotment a human being is entitled at least to hope for. However, due to the disclosure of the genetic information on him or her, nothing will ever be the same again.

If and when the problems predicted by the genetic warning show themselves in that person's life they are now her or his responsibility in a different way than if they had shown up without any kind of genetic forewarning, namely as the normal hazards of life. If e.g. a pregnant woman belonging to a special risk group chooses not to accept the offer of foetal diagnosis and selective abortion then the handicapped child, to whom she eventually gives birth, is not only her responsibility being the child's mother: she is, in her own as well as in other people's eyes, responsible not only for the handicapped child, but for having a child that is handicapped. It could have been avoided. As she did not use the option created by the genetic service the new situation is her own choice (Dworkin, 1988, chap. 5). Much the same goes for all the other kinds of life problems met by persons who either choose to ignore the genetic warnings or find themselves unable to follow the instructions coming together with the warning.

Thus it seems quite controversial whether the disclosure of genetic findings to unsuspecting persons is to be thought of as an enhancement of autonomy. In many cases of the kinds considered here it is rather misleading to think of them as cases where a person has a number of long-term preferences for herself or himself and then receives some useful, although maybe also worrying, information by the help of which he or she is put in a situation better to steer a safe way towards preference satisfaction, avoiding some blind ends, uncharted cliffs and unhelpful projects. One could instead argue that in many such cases what were initially very valuable options for the person to choose (for one set of reasons) or not to choose (for a different set of reasons) were being closed due to the disclosure. Of course, the option still remained open for the person, but the reason why he or she did not choose it was not that another one was considered more valuable. The reason was that she or he could not take the responsibility for choosing it, i.e. choosing it being aware of the genetic warning, because it would be a morally wrong thing to do, e.g. start building a family knowing in advance what kind of suffering this project of one's is bound to create for other people. Where the person concerned was formerly pondering the various options for trying to make something worthwhile out of life, accepting the normal hazards of life, she or he may now be struggling for moral survival. And as a result of this the history of that person's life may very well not be the history of an autonomous life, a life whose contents, for a significant part, are freely chosen among different and morally valuable alternatives. The history of that person's life might rather come to resemble the life of the person who had to become an electrician in order not to have to murder someone else - a life of morally forced choices.

Moralism as well as paternalism?

In their discussions of the duty to disclose and the right to know both the Nuffield Report and Ruth Macklin give pride of place to the interest of family members to be made fully aware of available information which would play a part in making important life decisions. However, it now seems that there might also be quite another interest of family members, *viz* the interest of making important life decisions without the interference of genetic information on themselves and their prospects in life. Perhaps it could even be argued, appealing to the right of autonomy, that people have a right to do so, thus also having a right not to know, not to be told and not to be approached unwittingly by benevolent relatives or medical services.

Remarkably, the Nuffield Report as well Ruth Macklin take for granted that the relative should be presented with the information that has become available. They argue that health professionals should seek to persuade individuals, if persuasion should be necessary, to allow the disclosure of relevant genetic information to other family members (Nuffield Council on Bioethics, 1993, p. 53, Macklin, 1992, p. 164). In its list of key ethical principles of genetic counselling the Nuffield Report first insists that counselling at each stage of the process should be non-directive, as far as possible. It then goes on to stipulate as one of the key ethical principles that the assurance of confidentiality should be coupled with an emphasis on the responsibility of individuals with a positive (abnormal) result to inform partners and family members (Nuffield Council on Bioethics, 1993, p. 37). The background of this principle is the following consideration:

> As a starting point, we adopt the view that a person acting responsibly would normally wish to communicate important genetic information to other family members who may have an interest in that information, and that a responsible person would normally wish to receive that information, particularly where it may have a bearing on decisions which he or she may be called upon to take in the future (Nuffield Council on Bioethics, 1993, p. 49).

It has already been argued that the decision to take the decision whether to know or not to know out of the unwitting family member's hands can be characterised as strongly paternalistic in relation to that person. It now seems difficult to avoid the impression that moralism is added to paternalism. According to the above the health professional should tell the patient what her or his moral duty is in relation to a third person. If necessary, the health professional should enlighten the patient on what the concept of a responsible person amounts to in the context of applied human genetics. So, on the one hand the professional should avoid any kind of directiveness in counselling on medical options, possibilities, probabilities etc., and, on the other hand, should be strongly directive in her or his counselling on general ethical matters and specific human relations on which the professional has no professional expertise at all.

Notes

1 cf. R. Dworkin's discussion of this point in Dworkin, R., (1993), chap. 8.
2 For further discussions of autonomy as self-determination cf. Dworkin, R., (1993), chap. 8, Dworkin, G., (1988), Raz, J., (1986), chap. 14, and Lindley, (1986).

References

Berlin, I. (1969), *Two Concepts of Liberty*, Clarendon Press: Oxford.

Brock, D. (1993), *Life and Death*, Cambridge University Press: Cambridge.

Dworkin, G. (1988), *The Theory and Practice of Autonomy*, Cambridge University Press: Cambridge.

Dworkin, R. (1993), *Life's Dominion*, Harper Collins Publishers: London.

Hare, R.M., (1994), 'Utilitarianism and Deontological Principles', in Gillon, R. (ed.), *Principles of Health Care Ethics*, pp. 149-159, John Wiley and Sons: Chichester.

Harris, J., (1985), *The Value of Life*, Routledge: London.

Lindley, R., (1986), *Autonomy*, MacMillan: London.

Macklin, R, (1992), 'Privacy and Control of Genetic Information', in Annas, G.J, and Elias, S. (eds), *Gene Mapping*, Oxford University Press: Oxford.

Nuffield Council on Bioethics, (1993), *Genetic Screening-Ethical Issues,* Nuffield Council on Bioethics: London.

Raz, J. (1986), *The Morality of Freedom*, Oxford University Press: Oxford.

7 Do 'all men desire to know'? A right of society to choose not to know about the genetics of personality traits

Darren Shickle

A devil, a born devil, on whose nature
Nurture can never stick (Prospero Tempest Act IV Scene 1)

The high prestige that science enjoys in our modern world is largely attributable to the many forms of technology that have had a major impact on the way we live our lives.   With a few exceptions, these new technologies have been advantageous, although the value placed on this utility may be subjective. Many new advances have provided a trigger for new research tools or strategies leading to an exponential increase in scientific enquiry.
   According to Hemple:

> apart from aiding man in his search for control over his environment, science answers another, disinterested, but no less deep and persistent urge: namely to gain ever wider knowledge and ever deeper understanding of the world in which he finds himself (1966, p. 2).

The other papers within this book have largely dealt with tensions between the rights of individuals to know or not to know. However, similar tensions arise at a population level. The scientific community may wish to exercise their right to conduct research to answer a particular hypothesis. There may be a right of the scientist to strive to find such knowledge, but the dissemination of the findings may threaten the ability of society to remain ignorant about areas of human life that at present may be best left unchallenged. One area of scientific endeavour of particular concern is genetic research which will potentially threaten our concept of personal identity and the integrity of the self.

Boorse drew an analogy between the ideal state of human health and a 1965 Volkswagen, which is in perfect mechanical condition when it conforms 'in all respects to the designer's detailed specifications' (Boorse, 1981, p.553). Presumably, theologians would argue that the various holy books of the world religions represent such divine manuals for human health. Medical science is still working on its version, although the final chapters are now being written.

Although Boorse's analogy has been criticised, it does hold in at least one aspect. The 1965 Volkswagon is an example of a model of car which has achieved 'vintage status'. However, our expectations of the 'state-of-the-art' car have changed over the years as we come to expect better performance and more features within the standard specification. In the same way, expectations of human performance have changed, whether it be the ability to run faster, live longer or to have greater intelligence. It is likely that some members of society may wish to use the technology that is available in order to ensure that aspirations are achieved. However, a society comprising of 'idealised clones' may not be desirable, if only because that this would lose an evolutionary advantage resulting from diversity. In order to avoid such a 'nightmare scenario' it may be necessary to place constraints on the states and conditions for which genetic technology can be used, and hence on the ability of individuals to exercise their autonomy.

Within existing medical practice there are examples of the dangers of 'unrestrained' autonomy. Couples are already requesting termination of pregnancy for conditions associated with reasonably normal quality of life. Consider a fetus diagnosed as having cleft lip and palate where there is a small risk (in the order of one percent) of associated tracheo-oesophageal fistula. Following counselling the parents request termination of pregnancy. However, there may be doubts as to the moral justification for this termination. Is it because the parents do not want a child with cleft lip and palate, even though surgical repair is likely to give a good cosmetic result? If the parents chose termination because of the risk of tracheo-oesophageal fistula, is one percent a sufficiently high risk?

Ruth Chadwick has pointed out 'that autonomous decision-making itself cannot be the only criterion of success' (1993, p.45). Autonomy must also be balanced against the other principles of biomedical ethics: beneficence, nonmaleficence and justice. On a practical level, scarcity of resources means that we cannot allow individuals to have all the health care that they want, irrespective of its cost and effectiveness.

Research within the 'New Genetics' has meant that a genetic aetiology is being recognised of many diseases not previously included within the domain of medical genetics. For some patients with cancer or heart disease, the strong family history means that a mendelian inheritance pattern can be identified.

70

However, a weaker family history exists for other patients which suggests that they have inherited one or more genes which meant that they were more susceptible to some other aetiological environmental or lifestyle factor. A genetic component is now recognised or suggested for many diseases e.g. breast cancer, bowel cancer, diabetes, and asthma (Ford and Easton, 1995; Cunningham and Dunlop, 1994; Aitman and Todd, 1995 and Cookson, 1994). A genetic aetiology has also been suggested for various forms of mental illness. In a population survey, Baird et al. (1988) found that 5.5 percent of the population would develop a genetic or part-genetic disorder by the age of 25, and 60 percent in a lifetime, when common disorders with multiple gene predisposition were included.

Genetic factors have also been suggested to be causal or contributory for various personality or cosmetic traits which have, until now, been considered to be variations of normality e.g. intelligence, homosexuality, obesity and aggression (Herrnstein and Murray, 1994; Burr, 1996; Bouchard and Perusse, 1993 and Horgan, 1993). Discovery of genes controlling such states could potentially lead to demands for gene therapy to modify them. However, interventions of this sort will change the boundaries of disease and normality.

While the new technology is valuable in reducing morbidity from genetic and other diseases in the population, drawing attention to differences between individuals and highlighting the mechanism for these variations is potentially dangerous. Many of us may wish to be more intelligent, to be more attractive physically, to be stronger or fitter but at present, our ability to alter these factors is limited and may involve considerable effort, through study, plastic surgery, or exercise. It could be argued that if parents are allowed to spend money on music lessons for their children, why should they not be allowed to pay for their child to have a gene for musicality inserted by gene therapy, if this became available at a future date. If technology was able to fulfil all our other desires, for example, of having blond, blue eyed children then the world would be very boring. Variation is a strength, even if only for evolutionary purposes. It is a statistical fact that half of the population will always be below the median, whether it be for height, intelligence, etc. Despite our effort to be in the upper percentile, the normal distribution means that this will never be possible, and all that will happen is that the overall population mean will go up: moving the goal posts for our aspirations.

There is a real danger that if the technology to modify personality traits became available then there would be some members of society that would want to use it. Indeed there may be subtle pressures for all to make use of it, just as Angus Clarke has identified with the non-directiveness of genetic counselling (1991). The very fact that the health care system offers a screening programme implies that the nature of the disease is such that an affected fetus should be terminated.

How may such a catastrophe be prevented? Is there a right of society not to know about the genetic basis of intelligence, gender etc.? Within the philosophical literature there seems to be an overwhelming consensus that knowledge is good. Aristotle actually begins his work on Metaphysics with the suggestion that: 'All men desire to know' (1991). Any knowledge seems to be considered good. Moral concerns are only raised when the way in which that knowledge is to be used is considered. Here we have the nub of the problem, if we think it is wrong to explore the genetics of intelligence for example, it is very difficult to stop the technology being used. We hope that nuclear weapons will never be used. We may strive to destroy them all, but the knowledge will always be available for a country to start building them again. They cannot be 'uninvented'. Of course, when scientists such as Marie Curie were conducting research on radioactivity at the turn of the century, they could not have been expected to have foreseen the horrors of Hiroshima and Nagasaki. The future use of nuclear weapons could only be prevented if a moratorium had been successfully imposed prior to some critical point in the path of their development.

There is a tension here between the rights of an individual whether it be an anxious parent or a scientist, to know and of society not to know. Glass proposed three commandments in the ethical basis of science (1966, p.89f.). The first was complete truthfulness and the second was 'thou shalt neither covet thy neighbour's ideas nor steal his experiments' (Glass, 1966, p.89). The third was somewhat different requiring, according to Glass, the fearless defence of intellectual freedom, 'for science cannot prosper where there is constraint upon daring thinking, where society dictates what experiments may be conducted, or where the statement of one's conclusions may lead to loss of livelihood, imprisonment, or even death'. Glass wrote that 'from the beginning the inveterate foe of scientific inquiry has been authority, whether this be the authority of tradition, of religion, or of the state'. However, there is a danger that science can itself become a dogma, itself assuming an authoritarian role, imposing itself on society.

Glass believed that 'science must be free to question and investigate any matter within the scope of its methods' (1966, p. 92). By wishing to prohibit research on personality traits we are interfering with the rights of the scientist to practice their trade. However, there is a duty on scientists to use their skills responsibly. The balancing of rights and duties has been enshrined in a number of statutes on human rights. For example the United Nations Universal Declaration of Human Rights (1948, article 29) indicates that the exercise of a person's rights and freedoms my be restricted for the purpose of meeting the 'just requirements of morality, public order and general welfare in a democratic society'. Similarly the European Convention on Human Rights (1950, article 8) states that a public authority in a democratic society may interfere with the exercise of an individual's rights if it is in the interests of national security, public safety or the economic well-being of the country, for the prevention of disorder or crime, for the protection of health and morals, or for the protection of the rights and freedoms of others.

Progress in scientific knowledge is similar to evolutionary change which is also generally irreversible. However, just as in the case of evolution one cannot say that all evolutionary change and natural selection is necessarily 'for the good of the species' (e.g. consider the fate of dinosaurs), so too it is necessary to question whether advancing knowledge is necessarily for the good of mankind. Applications of scientific advances in society nearly always create tensions and conflicts. It would indeed be a comfortable world, especially for the scientist, if we could simply let advancing evolution and science, going hand in hand, inevitably produce progress for the greater good of mankind, without our being concerned as to how they managed to do so. As Isaiah Berlin warns us there is danger in assuming 'that men will know more and therefore be wiser and better and happier'.

Popper (1973) drew a distinction between scientific revolutions and ideological revolutions. A theory, even a scientific theory, may become an entrenched ideology to the extent of becoming a substitute for religion. For example, the work of Copernicus and Darwin resulted in a scientific revolution. Both were responsible for overturning a dominant scientific theory. However in turn both gave rise to an ideological revolution by changing our view of our place in the universe. The ideological impact of Copernicus and Darwin was significant because each of them clashed with a religious dogma. In these cases, Popper described the ideological revolution as rational. However, he quoted quantum mechanics as an example of an ideological revolution arising out of scientific fashion which undermined rationality and provided an obstacle to the progress of science.

Popper quoted a number of scientific revolutions including Mendel's description of genetic inheritance, which he did not believe had been accompanied by ideological revolution. Writing in the early 1970s, Popper did not foresee an ideological revolution resulting from the breakthrough of Crick and Watson on the structure of DNA in 1953. There is a danger that research such as that on the genetics of personality traits will form an ideological revolution of the more destructive kind.

It may therefore be possible to draw a distinction between different forms of knowledge which generate different levels of moral concern. For example consider the Biblical story of the Garden of Eden. Among the many marvellous trees of the garden, the two which are singled out as being particularly important are the tree of life and the tree of knowledge of good and evil. However, it is this latter tree of good and evil that plays the more important role in the Book of Genesis. There the acquiring of knowledge is portrayed as the chief ingredient of human sin. What then is this knowledge of good and evil which according to the Bible is not to be found in Paradise but only in Paradise lost? It cannot be merely moral discrimination, the ability to know what is right and wrong. Nor can it be simply the ability to distinguish between what is beneficial and useful and what is harmful and dangerous. How could God possibly wish the knowledge of such things be denied to mankind?

As the serpent forecast and as God himself admitted later, when Adam and Eve ate the fruit of the forbidden tree they became like God, knowing good and evil. In Samuel 2 chapter 14, verse 17 the wise woman of Tekoa praises Absalom for having wisdom 'like the angel of God to discern good and evil ... to know all things that are on earth'. It is therefore the kind of knowledge that belongs to divinity, to the angels and ultimately to God himself, that is forbidden to humanity, the kind of full and comprehensive knowledge that brings to its owner power and independence. Francis Bacon said that 'knowledge is power'. The story in Genesis makes no distinction between the possession of knowledge and the use to which it is put. Humans are being told that they must not set their sights on divine status, but should remember their mortality and their dependence upon God for everything they have. This is a hard message for our modern age when our insatiable search for knowledge is almost universally commended.

Kierkegaard was happy to let science deal with plants and animals and stars. 'But to handle the spirit of man in such a fashion,' he wrote, 'is blasphemy'. Thus, it is possible to raise objections, not to science as such, but only to an attempt to extend the reign of science beyond its proper sphere. It is the limits of this sphere that requires further discussion.

The use of moratoria within genetics

There have been precedents for the use of moratoria within genetics. For example, in July 1974, a letter from the Committee on Recombinant DNA Molecules Assembly of Life Sciences with the USA National Academy of Sciences published a letter in *Science* (Berg, Baltimore, Boyer et al., 1974) making a number of recommendations as to the type of procedures which should not be followed concluding that their:

> concern for the possible unfortunate consequences of indiscriminate application of these techniques motivates us to urge all scientists working in this area to join us in agreeing not to initiate experiments ... until attempts have been made to evaluate the hazards and some resolution of the outstanding questions has been achieved.

This moratorium was observed internationally for a period of seven months and terminated in 1975 (Berg, Baltimore, Brenner, Roblin and Singer, 1975). It has been suggested that a major factor, if not in the setting up of the moratorium, at least in the uniform observance of it, was a desire to retain information within the scientific community until a sufficiently sanitised scientific stratagem could be released for public consumption. If this is the case, then this example so often quoted by the scientific community as evidence of their social responsibility and accountability, may be somewhat misleading.

More recently, the Clothier Report (1992, para. 4.15) on the use of gene therapy within the UK, has placed a moratorium on the use of germ-line gene therapy. While somatic gene therapy was permitted, the Committee felt that there was sufficient uncertainty about possible side-effects of germ-line gene therapy for future generations. In addition, the birth of affected children could be avoided by other means e.g. genetic testing of in-vitro fertilised fetuses.

There are of course substantial weaknesses with the idea of using moratoria to regulate scientific development. The initial attraction of the idea is the comprehensive nature of the prohibition, but this is also perhaps the inherent weakness. Completely forbidding an activity frustrates the inquisitive aspect of human nature and invites breach. This is particularly the case since those forbidden in this instance are scientists and researchers whose reputations and livelihoods depend on constantly moving the corpus of knowledge forward. In practice, a moratorium could be introduced by removing state funding for research in prohibited areas. This would still allow funding from private resources or industry. However, if society has expressed ethical concerns about such research it is unlikely that they would be willing to risk the bad publicity from funding such research. Moratoria are also by their nature susceptible to practical difficulties. What sanctions are to be imposed on those who breach the moratorium, who should enforce them and with what authority? The difficulty with this as a means of regulating something as profoundly troubling as genetics is that it does not operate at a level much beyond that of relying on the conscience of the individual.

It could be argued that if research raises ethical concerns, then it may be better for it to be performed by scientists who also share ethical concerns, under an explicit regulatory mechanism, subject to public scrutiny. However, this argument is similar to that used by Western countries to justify selling weapons to the developing countries: if we do not sell them then somebody else will, and it is better that we get the business and also know who has bought the weapons. However, this argument does not make the arms trade any more morally acceptable. During the height of the Cold War, there was a debate within most European countries about unilateral versus multilateral nuclear disarmament. It was claimed that for one country to give up their nuclear weapons unilaterally would be a futile gesture, and would leave that country open to the nuclear threats of an enemy.

By placing a unilateral moratorium on genetic research into personality traits, a country may miss out on the prestige associated with a scientific breakthrough, and indeed the commercial advantages that may go with it. There may also be very real benefits from associated research that could be foregone. For example, research on the genetics of intelligence would be advantageous if it were to explain the causes of mental handicap and to produce new therapies. However, if a society thinks that something is wrong, then it should say so and act accordingly, even if it is a futile gesture. If however, we do not wish to go as far as a moratorium, are there any other actions that we should take?

The proper application of scientific research will not happen unless both the scientist and non-scientist consider the potential moral problems that arise. While scientist are likely to know most about the technical aspects of an application, they do not have a monopoly on the ability to consider ethical consequences. Indeed, self interest, even if altruistic, may mean that scientists will not be the best people to do so, although there will be a duty on scientists to inform this debate. In a survey of consumer attitudes to the use of biotechnology in agriculture and food production, 85 percent of the public agreed or strongly agreed that 'citizens deserve a great role in decisions about science and technology', and 82 percent felt that citizens have too little say on deploying biotechnology (Rolin, 1995). At present, the quality of education in science that most members of the population have received may mean that a widespread debate will be difficult. The media will therefore have an important role in providing the public with an understanding of scientific issues, so that applications create less of a problem simply due to misunderstanding. This should also allow all members of society to help make sensible assessments as to what should be done about applications of scientific advances.

If society wishes to permit genetic research on personality traits, so be it, provided that this has been after a meaningful debate in which costs and benefits are discussed. At present, most of the public are ignorant of the direction of genetic research and its potential costs and benefits. In this context, the public have a right to know what research is being conducted, at which point they may choose to exercise a right not to know. At a time of scarce resources for health care, let alone medical research, funds should be directed at alleviating diseases and abnormality, rather that creating new ones.

References

Aitman, T.J. and Todd, J.A. (1995), 'Molecular Genetics of Diabetes Mellitus', *Baillieres Clinical Endocrinology and Metabolism,* Vol. 9, No. 3, pp. 631-56.

Aristotle (1991), *The Metaphysics*, trans. McMahon, J.H, Buffalo: Prometheus Books.

Baird, P.A., Anderson, T.W., Newcombe, H.B. and Lowry, R.B, (1988), 'Genetic Disorders in Children and Young Adults: A Population Study', *American Journal of Human Genetics*, No. 42, pp. 677-93.

Berg, P., Baltimore, D., Boyer, H.W., et al. (1974), 'Potential Biohazards of Recombinant DNA Molecules', *Science,* No. 185, pp. 303.

Berg, P., Baltimore, D., Brenner, S., Roblin, R.O. and Singer, M.F. (1975), 'Asilomar Conference on Recombinant DNA Molecules', *Science,* No. 188 pp. 991-4.

Boorse, C. (1981), 'On the Distinction Between Disease and Illness', in Caplan, A.L., Engelhart, H.T., and McCartney, J.J. (eds), *Concepts of Health and Disease*, pp. 545-60, Addison-Wesley Publishing Company: Massachusetts.

Bouchard, C. and Perusse, L. (1993), 'Genetic Aspects of Obesity', *Annals of the New York Academy of Sciences*, No. 699, pp. 26-35.

Burr, C. (1996), *A Separate Creation*, Hyperion: New York.

Chadwick, R.F. (1993), 'What Counts as Success in Genetic Counselling?' *Journal of Medical Ethics*, Vol. 19, No. 1, pp. 43-46.

Clarke, A. (1991), 'Is Non-directive Genetic Counselling Possible?', *Lancet*, No. 338, pp. 998-1001.

Clothier Report (1992), *Report of the Committee on the Ethics of Gene Therapy* (Clothier Report), Cm.1788, HMSO: London.

Cookson, W. (1994), 'Atopy: A Complex Genetic Disease', *Annals of* Medicine, Vol. 26, No. 5, pp. 351-3.

Council of Europe, Convention for the Protection of Human Rights and Fundamental Freedoms, (1950, article 8). in Council of Europe, (1992), *Human Rights in International Law: Basic texts*, Council of Europe Press: Strasbourg.

Cunningham, C. and Dunlop, M.G. (1994), 'Genetics of Colorectal Cancer', *British Medical Bulletin*, Vol. 50, No. 3, pp. 640-55.

Ford, D. and Easton, D.F. (1995), 'The Genetics of Breast and Ovarian Cancer', *British Journal of Cancer*, Vol. 72, No. 4, pp. 805-12.

Glass, B. (1966), *Science and Ethical Values*, The University of North Carolina Press: Chapel Hill.

Hempel, C.G. (1966), *Philosophy of Natural Science*, Prentice-Hall: Englewood Cliffs.

Herrnstein, R. and Murray, C. (1994), *The Bell Curve*, The Free Press: New York.

Horgan, J. (1993) 'Genes and Crime. A US Plan to Reduce Violence Rekindles an Old Controversy', *Scientific American*, Vol. 268, No. 2, pp. 24-29.

Popper, K. (1973), *Objective Knowledge: An Evolutionary Approach*, Claredon Press: Oxford.

Rolin, B.E. (1995), *The Frankenstein Syndrome*, Cambridge University: Cambridge.

United Nations. United Nations Universal Declaration of Human Rights (1948, article 29) in Council of Europe, (1992), *Human Rights in International Law: Basic texts*, Council of Europe Press: Strasbourg.

8 Mass media and public discussion in bioethics

Ruth Chadwick and Mairi Levitt

Besides printing the news, papers also teach by their stories that doctors are curing cancer (Ivan Illich)

Introduction

An examination of sources of public information on advances in genetics is central to the 'right to know' debate. Calls are made with increasing frequency for raising public awareness of issues in bioethics - the report of the Nuffield Council on Bioethics on genetic screening is one example. This has important practical significance, for as the Royal College of Physicians has pointed out:

> The influences most responsible for the substantial improvement in ethical standards over the past two decades are probably peer pressure from other investigators and increased public awareness of medical ethics (Royal College of Physicians, 1990, para. 10.3)

The question to consider is the role of the media here: how successful are they in raising public awareness? As regards the medical developments themselves, do they portray too rosy a picture, giving rise to unrealistic expectations of, for example, in vitro fertilisation? Or do they foster fears that may prove to be groundless, as in the Frankenstein brand of reporting of genetic technology? Fnally, how do they facilitate public awareness of the ethical implications?

This paper will concentrate on one sector of the media, namely the press, and within that (for the most part but not exclusively) the quality press in the UK. It will also look at reporting of one issue in genetics, namely genetic screening. Results of a manual search of coverage, dating from 1982, will be discussed. It will be shown that this search suggests a gradual move from an early enthusiasm when new techniques are first reported, to a more balanced approach which recognises the problems. Despite the generally greater awareness of problems, the transition from uncritical acceptance to discussion of the pros and cons is still made for each new technique alongside more general reporting of the effects of the 'new genetics'.

Much greater concern has been displayed in discussions of bioethics over the implications of gene therapy, but it could be argued that genetic screening has the potential to do the greater harm. In the light of this, and of the popular wisdom that 'Prevention is better than cure' it is of particular interest to examine coverage of screening as part of the 'right to know' debate.

Genetic screening presented in a positive light

When developments in genetics first come to the attention of the media we found that the reporting tends to take an uncritical stance, reporting the 'breakthrough', the new discovery or technique and its likely benefits with quotations from scientists and medical staff. The issues are simple at this stage - here is a new discovery, a revolutionary technique which will benefit people. On prenatal screening, a cutting from the start of the survey has the headline 'Take genes test, couples urged', and is an example of an early confident style with comments from a doctor but not from patients (The Guardian, 28.8.85). Bernadette Modell is quoted as saying: 'Couples should take prenatal gene tests to find out if they are at risk of having handicapped babies by passing on genetic defects'. The article paints a picture of the heavy burden of handicap for the patient, family and whole community, and predates political correctness in its terminology. Similar positive comments, greeting new techniques enthusiastically with medical opinion reported unquestioningly, include 'New Down's test avoids risk to foetus' and 'soon we can offer [young mothers] risk-free foetal analysis' (The Sunday Observer, 25.9.94).

The tests themselves are described as 'a simple blood test', 'an ordinary blood sample' which are 'risk free' and will benefit many. *The Independent*, for example, (16.3.93) reported on a 'blood test ... to identify women at risk of cancer'. GPs were urged to consider the possibility that some families might have an inherited predisposition and women who suspected that they were members of an affected family were recommended to seek advice. There was no discussion of the ethical issues at this stage - 'solutions' were described as follows by a Professor who co-ordinated the international study:

> the at-risk women could decide to have healthy breasts and healthy ovaries removed in their thirties and forties ... [this will be] a very personal decision ... the decision is not so much to do with the risks, more to do with how she can cope (The Independent 16.3.93).

No potential patient was asked to comment.

This phenomenon is perhaps to be expected, given that the medical profession is the *source* of the information about new techniques. Anne Karpf, in *Doctoring the Media*, writes that:

> The medical profession occupies a peculiar position vis-à-vis the mass media ... no other profession, except politicians, is so frequently depicted, and itself so consistently provides access, interviews, and speakers (Karpf, 1988, p. 110).

In addition, there is evidence to suggest that the timing of the release to the public of information is carefully controlled by the medical profession (Shickle, 1993) and that those who disagree with the prevailing view find it difficult to make their voices heard, as in the case of David Wainwright Evans in his claims about 'deception' on organ donor cards (Evans, 1994). Shickle, in particular, discussed the argument that it is considered undesirable to alarm the public (e.g., in a public health scare such as reported in the UK in 1994 with headlines such as 'Killer bug ate my face') and shows that while paternalism might be outmoded in the clinical encounter, it continues to flourish in relation to informing the public.

Negative coverage of genetic screening

Once specific programmes are underway in the UK the benefits are no longer seen as so obvious - experience is more complicated than predicted. Reports incorporate patient experience as well as medical evidence On the assumed benefits of screening generally: headlines have read 'spotting tiny flaws in our DNA will not make our health problems vanish overnight'; (The Sunday Observer, 10.10.93); and 'Warning: Government screening programmes could seriously damage your health', (The Sunday Times magazine, 8.10.94), and on breast cancer screening; 'this breakthrough could raise more problems than it solves'. The 'simple' tests are seen to be not 100 percent effective: a mother is quoted: 'A false positive made my pregnancy a misery' (Mother and Baby, July 1994). The burden on women to make a decision for or against testing is recognised; screening creates anxiety and tests 'will never be able to identify every woman carrying a Down's child' (The Times, 30.1.96).

Ethical issues

Not surprisingly, it is in the negative coverage that the ethical issues begin to be discussed. That may be because ethical *issues* are interpreted as ethical *problems*, although even when a new development is presented as positive there are ethical issues to discuss, such as access. In early coverage of a new advance it is taken-for-granted that it will benefit people in general, by offering greater knowledge and choice; there is no need for an ethical debate, but when the technique is actually used the 'people in general' become specific individuals for whom knowledge and choice bring ethical dilemmas.

The article on breast cancer screening cited above quoted a family member as saying: 'There's too much we can inherit - who wants to know?' British MP Brian Wilson, parent of a child with Down's syndrome, says 'I cannot accept an ethos which assumes it to be an undisputed social good for Down's syndrome babies to be detected in the womb, only in order that they might be more effectively disposed of' (The Guardian, 7.12.93).

Both these quotations raise the question: what actually is the point of screening? What happens once you have the knowledge? They make it clear that a simple association of screening with prevention is inadequate. The value of knowledge about genetics, earlier welcomed as facilitating choice, is questioned e.g. the article *The cloud of knowing* (The Independent on Sunday, 14.2.94). Worries are expressed about the consequences of information for individual lives. In some cases having the knowledge does not necessarily bring with it scope for action, and when it does, the action in question may be unacceptable to some, e.g. abortion. When having a handicapped baby was generally unavoidable it was also assumed to be undesirable or even tragic for the family concerned; once choices are beginning to be available new questions arise; for example, does society want to eliminate Down's syndrome?[1] Questioning of whether abortion in cases of genetic disorder is a good thing (other than by those opposed to abortion under any circumstances) is accompanied by a more positive view of Down's syndrome babies in particular. Testimony by mothers who chose to have their baby because they 'feel [they] can cope' features nationally known figures, such as the wife of Damon Hill the racing driver, almost always with 'photogenic' young children.

A story of a woman aged 34 suing an obstetrician at a private hospital for £1 million because she was not offered the predictive blood test and had a Down's syndrome baby is not in the 'poor patient suffering from doctor's error' category but evokes an article in response to the 'right to a perfect baby' which concludes that 'a society where only normal children were born would be emotionally impoverished' and condemns the use of 'expensive, unnecessary and anxiety-raising tests' in the USA 'purely for legal reasons' (The Independent, 24.8.92).

The questioning of the desirability of 'therapeutic' abortion regularly brings forth the phrases 'designer babies' and the question of 'when and how to draw the line'. *The Independent on Sunday* claims 'the age of the designer baby is probably less than two decades away' (18.7.93), ten years after *The Observer* predicted that 'designer-made babies could become as fashionable tomorrow as designer-made jeans today'. It is interesting to note that the term 'designer babies' is almost always incorporated in negative reporting, normally without an explanation being offered as to why the idea of design in this context should be thought undesirable.

Fears about the abuse of screening to eliminate so-called 'undesirables' are likely to refer to Nazi Germany or, less frequently to USA sterilisation programmes. In an article entitled *'Sceptre of Nazi Values'* a Human Genome Project scientist calls for legislation against discrimination and quotes a spokeswoman for the Project as saying it does not raise ethical issues itself but 'society has to decide what it is prepared to have happen' (The Guardian, 8.4.93).

Who benefits from new knowledge and technology?

The quotation from Brian Wilson above brings into the public arena the question of what counts as a social good in relation to screening. Other reports have pointed to the need for control over genetic screening because of commercial pressures and the potential for use of genetic information by employers and insurance companies. Attention to this issue may be partly due to the AIDS experience.

There was evidence of a marked degree of concern expressed about the commercial pressures involved in the move to greater use of genetic screening. The motives and power of scientists are questioned. The headline 'Gods who are selling our genes' reports on the International Congress of Genetics and the financial rewards available for those who exploit genetic discoveries. An article in *The Independent* pointed to 'a massive unspoken assumption that once people see and understand what the scientists are doing, they will approve' (19.8.93).

Another article reflects points that have been made recently in the bioethical literature about a new genetic orthodoxy, or 'geneticization' as Abby Lippman calls it (Lippman, 1994, p. 13). A new orthodoxy is mentioned: that literally any illness must be curable, and that the pre-emptive strike has become a mass preoccupation. The same article suggests that criticism is difficult because programmes are already in place and 'empires have been constructed' - GPs are locked into the system (The Sunday Times Magazine, 8.10.94).

Media ethics

Our analysis has shown a gradual shift from naive reporting of advances in genetic screening to more critical coverage. So how successful are the media we have considered in raising public awareness? We have not of course compared them with other media such as television, which in addition to reporting has the facility for 'Hypotheticals' and dramatisation. What needs to be considered, however, is how successful the press is in terms of what its own goals are (or perhaps should be).

The goal of newsworthiness is significant in this context   There are conventions about what is newsworthy, and new medical developments fall into this category. This is precisely why the medical profession is the most highly represented after politicians. Karpf (1988) points to the importance of two general types of story that retain their value as newsworthy: the moral panic story and the miracle cure; the threat to society versus its redemption. This has to compete, however, with the convention of 'destroying the hero', which is not entirely confined to the British Royal Family and occurs in the reporting of genetics. The attitude of awe at the advances made by scientists changes to a more cynical stance. In 'Rocks on the path to the DNA grail' (The Observer 10.10.93) the reporter 'ponders the claim that we are being conned with pledges of miracle cures' and acknowledges that 'part of the problem is that scientists in seeking public approbation and funds, are willing to fall in with the journalistic hunger for uncomplicated truths'.

What then *should* they be doing? Klaidman and Beauchamp (1992) have argued that 'What the press have a duty to report is roughly correlated with what the public has a need to know'.

To elucidate this they develop a model of a reasonable reader who has 'needs for information about matters such as the risks, alternatives, and consequences of what is being reported'.

These categories of information, *viz* risks, alternatives and consequences, are arguably of particular relevance in the context of a medical intervention such as genetic screening. If Klaidman and Beauchamp are right, it might suggest the need for a 'balanced' approach.

We did find some evidence of what might be called balanced reporting in so far as attempts were made to present both sides of the argument. *Mother and Baby* magazine (July 1994) gave what purported to be a factual account of tests available and followed this with accounts from mothers with positive and negative feelings about them. We also found an attempt to compare 'good' and 'bad' precedents in genetic screening - Tay-Sachs versus sickle-cell programmes.

Klaidman and Beauchamp also raise the question, however, of what counts as a balanced account. Using the example of stories involving complex decisions about medical ethics, they say:

> nonphysician reporters covering complex stories ... cannot be expected to be more expert than highly specialized physicians or ethicists. So how should they present the range of views to provide readers with the most objective account possible? Should they include every viewpoint and let readers make their own diagnoses, prognoses, and evaluations? One difficulty with such an approach ... is that most readers ... like most journalists, are ill equipped to make such judgements (Klaidman and Beauchamp, 1987, p. 47).

Whatever view one takes on the last comment, their provisional conclusion seems right: that the reader should be made aware of 'the central knowable truth of the situation: uncertainty and a range of informed to uninformed speculation'.

To the arguments against paternalism in medical ethics there are analogous arguments against paternalism in conveying information about medical developments to the public - individuals may be influenced into making significant life choices on the basis of such information. Raising public awareness thus requires information about complexity. The survey conducted for this article did not point the finger at journalists for oversimplifying the issues. The early simplistic reports contained information from the scientists themselves, and were similar to reports in popular scientific journals in terms of findings and applications. In later stories on the same development a wider range of views are available and used by the journalists. In fact on the issue we chose to look at we found the range of arguments in the press to be a fair representation of those in the bioethics literature, exploring ethical dilemmas and conflicts of interest rather than simply teaching that 'doctors cure cancer'.

Notes

1   In the media the presentation of a genetic disorder varies according to context. There are both positive success stories about a Down's girl passing her driving test and news of a new, early and less risky method of screening for Down's with a paragraph on the parents of a 3 year old Down's boy who 'has yet to speak'. Both these stories are true but it would be uncomfortable to remind people about the achievements of someone with a disorder for which most mothers choose termination. Here the media is echoing the approach of genetic counsellors. Research has shown that the pre-test information given to parents 'is largely negative' as it presents a story 'oriented to avoiding the birth of a child with Down's syndrome' whereas after-birth information 'tends to be more positive' and is 'oriented to caring for a child' with the condition (Lippman and Wilfond, 1992, p. 936). The authors ask whether the same story should be told to families considering testing before birth and those receiving a postnatal diagnosis.

References

Belsey, A. and Chadwick, R. (eds), (1992), *Ethical Issues in Journalism and the Media*, Routledge: London.
Durrant, J., Anders H., Bauer, M., Gosling, A. (1993), *The Human Genome Project and the British Public*, (Final Report to the European Commission of a research project 'Public Awareness and Media Coverage of the Human Genome Project in Britain').
Evans, D.W. (1994), 'Brain Stem Death - a Deception', *Philosophy Today*, No. 12, pp. 1-2.

Karpf, A. (1988), *Doctoring the Media: The Reporting of Health and Medicine,* Routledge: London.

Klaidman, S. and Beauchamp, T.L. (1987), *The Virtuous Journalist,* Oxford University Press: New York.

Lippman, A. (1994), 'The Genetic Construction of Prenatal Testing', Rothenberg, K.H. and Thomson E.J. (eds) *Women and Prenatal Testing Facing the Challenges of Genetic Technology,* Ohio State University Press: Columbus.

Lippman, A. and Wilfond, B.S. (1992), 'Twice-told Tales: Stories about Genetic Disorders', *American Journal of Human Genetics,* Vol. 51, pp. 936-937.

Nuffield Council on Bioethics, (1993), *Genetic Screening Ethical Issues,* Nuffield Council on Bioethics: London

Royal College of Physicians, (1990), *Research Involving Patients,* Royal College of Physicians of London.

Shickle, D. (1993), *A Moral Perspective on the Withholding of Information About Patulin Contamination of Apple Juice from the Public,* Unpublished essay.

9 Living with the future: Genetic information and human existence

Henk ten Have

Genetic information and the media

The media are frequently drawing our attention to genetic discoveries. These reports seem to follow a particular pattern: the gene mutation associated with a particular disease has been identified; an effective therapy for the disease is lacking, and it is not probable that the discovery itself will enhance the development of therapeutic possibilities. However, the discovery will lead to more or less accurate prediction of the presence and prognosis of the disease when individuals are tested, even long before the onset of symptoms.

An example of such a reporting pattern occurred when the genetics research group in Nijmegen University announced that they had isolated the genetic structure responsible for Steinert's disease. This is one of the most frequent muscular dystrophies, occurring in 1 out of 8000 persons. It is characterised by weakness of limb muscles and facial muscles. Onset is very variable, but for many patients it may be as late as the fourth decade. No cure is as yet available.

The discovery was published in a scientific journal but also widely reported in the media. In newspaper interviews the researchers pointed out the practical implications. Although this scientific breakthrough will not lead to any therapy, the researchers argued in *De Telegraaf* (6.2.92), that 'it makes it possible to detect the disease with hundred percent certainty long before the onset of the first symptoms'. Also the severity of the disease can be prognosticated from the extent of the abnormalities of the DNA.

Public representations of genetic research, following the above pattern, generate a complex set of questions regarding the impact and value of genetic knowledge. Focusing on the management of information on the level of the individual has a tendency within moral debate to neglect the social dimension of genetic information. Clarification of the right to know and the right not to know, although valuable in itself as a possible way to empower individual persons, also needs to elucidate the cultural context within which genetic knowledge is promulgated, as well as the social processes involved in the dissemination of genetic technologies. Communication of new genetic discoveries reveals a paradoxical tension between knowledge and application. On the one hand, researchers publish the results of their projects because knowledge in itself is valuable. One of the rationales for the Human Genome Project is that it will lead to gains in basic knowledge. On the other hand and at the same time it is stipulated that genetic research has potential for medical advancement. Publication of knowledge claims, especially in the public media, seems almost always to be accompanied by expositions of the potential practical implications and the relevancy to patient care.

The immediate linking of knowledge and application creates particular difficulties for moral debate. The fact that knowledge is available should not in itself dictate its application. What is necessary is prior identification of the goals that we want to accomplish in using the knowledge, a careful balancing of the benefits and harms generated through the application of knowledge, and a delineation of the norms and values that should be respected. Multiplication of technological possibilities therefore calls for a concomitant development of the moral framework which guides and regulates potential and actual applications of genetic technology.

In order to promote human use of new technologies, ethical reflection will be unavoidable. At the same time, such reflection is already more or less oriented to particular applications since these are pre-given and postulated together with the knowledge claims.

The intertwinement of knowledge and application claims also calls into question the responsibility of the human genetics community to communicate clearly and accurately the nature and significance of genetic information. Sometimes communication is overstated, for example when it is claimed that the Human Genome Project will provide the ultimate answers to the chemical underpinnings of human existence (Watson, 1990).

Moreover, such representation of genetic research can lead to particular public perceptions. It creates, for example, the impression that knowledge about many individual genes is knowledge about how the genome functions in people. It also leads to the fact, discussed by Fogle (1995), that genes are viewed by the public as entities, each of which controls one portion of the phenotype, rather than as integrated into a system.

The moral value of genetic information

The current development of genetics is a challenge, particularly to societies, to reflect upon the future evolution of human life and social existence. Genetic knowledge is not private information, but necessarily implies relatives. Genetic information is also valuable to third parties, such as insurance companies, employers, and prosecutors. Genetic technology can affect future generations. For these reasons, developing a framework of moral norms and regulations should involve all members of society. A crucial issue underlying this development concerns the moral value and meaning of genetic information. Obtaining more information is not necessarily better, unless there is a clear perception of the benefits, goals, or uses which may be approached or realised with such knowledge. The fact that genetic information is available for practical use does not imply that it is morally justified to actually use the knowledge. The morally relevant point is how to make meaningful use of the available genetic information. Various moral principles, rights and rules have been developed to delineate what is regarded as meaningful use. It is also possible to approach the issue from another perspective. Let us assume that the Human Genome Project has realised its claims: mapping of the human genome has been successful and all human genes have been located on the chromosomes. Diagnostic tests to identify all disease genes and predict any genetic dispositions and susceptibilities are flooding the health market. Assuming that the Genome Project has been ultimately and completely successful, we still have to concern ourselves with questions about the moral value of predictive knowledge of future human existence.

Geneticization

Prima facie, it seems unavoidable that the future will bring us a society within which all potentially useful genetic information is freely available and actually applied. In principle, every member of this society will be able to foretell his or her individual fate from reading his or her genes, and to adapt his or her personal life plan in accordance with such predictive knowledge.

In the opinion of critical authors such as Lippman (1992), this future has already partly begun. Society is involved in a process of geneticization. As an instance of the more encompassing process of medicalization, this process involves a redefinition of individuals in terms of DNA codes, a new language to describe and interpret human life and behaviour in a genomic vocabulary of codes, blueprints, traits, dispositions, genetic makeup, and a gentechnological approach to disease, health and the body. Popular culture in post-modern society is indeed pervaded with genetic imagery. Nelkin and Lindee (1995) examining popular sources such as television, radio talk shows, comic books and science fiction, show how popular images 'convey a striking picture of the gene as powerful, deterministic, and central to an understanding of both everyday behaviour and the 'secret of life' (1995, p. 2). It seems that the cultural meaning of DNA nowadays is remarkably similar to that of the immortal soul of Christian theology. The bio-information metaphor and cartographic metaphor, often used in the context of the genome project, are in fact reworkings of the mechanical metaphor that has been frequently used in the past in medical discourses on the body. These linguistic (and often also visual) representations of the body carry with them the importance of a technological approach: machinery is used to fix machinery. They represent the body as comprising 'a multitude of tiny interchangeable parts, rendering the body amenable to objectification and technological tinkering in the interest of developing the 'perfect' human' (Lupton, 1994, p. 61).

Development towards a geneticized future is apparently possible because of the consensus regarding two ideals in current moral debate: the ideal of value neutrality of clinical genetics and the ideal of individual responsibility in health matters.

Non-directiveness

One of the prime tenets of genetic counselling is patient autonomy. Once genetic information is available, the basic rule is that patients or clients should be able to use the information according to their personal views. Geneticists or counsellors should not seek to tell patients or clients whether they should obtain particular information or what they should do with the information if they acquire it. In other words, the goal of genetic counselling or screening is to inform patients or clients about what is possible and what their options are (Collins, 1991). The leading principle of counselling and screening therefore is non-directiveness. Accurate information should be provided to the person concerned regarding the nature of potential genetic conditions, the prognosis, possible treatments and preventive strategies. The experts providing such information should not, in any respect, try to influence the decisions made by the persons who are counselled or screened.

The moral ideal underlying this practice of clinical genetics is value-neutrality. The genetic expert is withholding any normative judgement regarding the obtaining and application of genetic information; his or her aim is merely to provide information and to help the patients or clients to work through possible options. It is evident that this ideal in itself is a weak counterbalance to tendencies to make genetic tests more generally accessible. Patient values are to be decisive whenever choices have to be made on the basis of genetic information. When respect for individual autonomy is the basic norm guiding the use of genetic information, it is also reasonable to expect that predictive 'combi-tests' will eventually be on sale in the supermarket or drugstore (De Wert, 1994).

A second determinant that may further increase the significance of genetic information is the ideal of individual responsibility for personal health. Health policy and health education, especially in times of limited budgets and reduced expenditures, increasingly appeal to the notion of 'personal responsibility'. If health policy defines a particular problem as undesirable, and if health education research shows the problem to be associated with a particular life-style, then health policy can attribute responsibility to those individuals that exhibit that life-style, particularly since life-style is supposedly the free choice of rational individuals.

Traditionally, in health care the rhetoric of responsibility is used in a specific way. In the medical model of disease, patients are usually not held responsible for the genesis and evolution of their illnesses. Diagnosing a condition as disease introduces excusability. When a person's condition is interpreted as illness, the medical judgement implies that he or she cannot be blamed for his or her condition, and that treatment and care are appropriate and morally desirable. In this traditional model, the notion of responsibility is used with prospective force: it is equivalent to saying that a person has an obligation to preserve his or her health. Through assigning responsibility to the individual for his or her future health, an attempt is made to guide and change the individual's behaviour. Such practical use of the concept is different from the retrospective ascription of responsibility. The latter use implies an evaluation of what has happened. If an individual has a health problem, he or she is held causally responsible because of his or her unhealthy life-style or risky behaviour in the past. This use combines causality with culpability. Since the person himself is the cause of his or her present problem, he or she is also answerable for the consequences of his or her prior behaviour. Retrospective use of the concept of responsibility therefore is retributive; it implies disapproval and blame.

In present-day health policy there seems to be a development towards connecting the prospective and retrospective sense of 'responsibility' (ten Have and Loughlin, 1994). Usually, the line of argumentation is as follows. If there is an urgent need to reduce the costs of health care, and if at the same time it is scientifically argued that major expenditures are associated with certain patterns of behaviour, it is tempting to create an obligation to be healthy and to introduce some system of sanction for those who do not implement such obligation. In a liberal society, individuals are normally free to do as they choose. In this respect, caring for your health is not different from other dimensions of personal life. But when individual choices turns out badly, and when individuals remain uninfluenced by moral appeals of health educators, legal and financial sanctions may be thought justified.

Today, a similar argument is used concerning predictive information. It may be prudent to use genetic diagnosis to predict future disabilities, and therefore appeals to (prospective) responsibility may be justified; but this argument in practice is often linked with the argument that individuals who deliberately have not used diagnostic possibilities, should be (retrospectively) responsible for adverse consequences for themselves or their offspring. When, for example, a couple decides not to use prenatal diagnosis, or not to terminate pregnancy in case of diagnosed fetal disorders, it is argued that the couple is then responsible for the suffering of the child, when indeed a child with handicaps is born (Hilhorst, 1993). If suffering could have been avoided, and a choice is made not to use predictive opportunities, parents should bear the consequences of their irresponsible choice; they can no longer argue that suffering has befallen them; they have themselves to blame.

This line of argumentation, if indeed taken seriously, will be a significant stimulus for individuals to obtain genetic information as much as possible, particularly when there is a threat that governments, insurance companies and employers will work with a system of incentives and disincentives. When there is a cultural imagery that future diseases, disorders and disabilities can be foretold by examining the individual's genome, persons can no longer claim that they are victims, if they have deliberately decided not to use predictive diagnosis. It has been their voluntary choice not to know, and not to eliminate potential disadvantages to their health.

A genetic civilisation strategy?

The ideals of value-neutrality of clinical genetics and of personal responsibility for health prevailing in current health ethics debate, may indeed generate a situation where the availability of genetic information in itself produces its wide-spread application. In this view, human beings in the next millennium will be dominated by predictive knowledge of their genome and driven by new norms in interpersonal behaviour.

Such an assumption is not unrealistic since we have witnessed a similar change in normative behaviour patterns at the close of the last century (ten Have, 1990). With the rise of new knowledge about the origin and transmission of infectious diseases, in many countries philanthropic activities have been organised to civilise the public through inculcating the new hygienic norms. Philanthropists launched a large scale offensive to civilise the habits and life-styles of the masses. As enlightened men, they coupled assistance with moralisation. Norms of behaviour, such as cleanliness, domestic nursing, and soberness were transmitted not by repression or coercion but by the subtle means of advice, persuasion and education. The result was the normalisation of individual behaviour. The new norms of a healthy, regular, and disciplined conduct passed into domestic life; the strategy succeeded in having the norms internalised. Hygienism thus produced a new behaviour pattern in the general population.

Why could a similar transformation of life-styles not occur today as a result of new genetic information? Though it is hard to forecast the future, two factors can be identified that may prevent, hinder or at least restrict this development towards geneticization of future human existence.

The first factor is the need to make some delineation between disease and health, normality and abnormality, given the uncontrollable wealth of information that will, in the end, be available. In current ethical debate, the above distinctions are increasingly problematic. It is apparently difficult to make use of these traditional distinctions in determining what conditions should be screened (or not). Perhaps it is even thought impossible to apply them as normative criteria guiding potential genetic screening programmes. Nonetheless, the exponential growth of genetic data and resulting possibilities of detection, will inevitably lead to an urgent need of selection; without selective use and meaningful criteria to make distinctions of value among the immense data available, the usefulness of data will be questionable. The multiplication of possibilities for testing will at the same time increase the necessity to reach consensus regarding those conditions and predispositions that seriously restrict the functioning of human beings within community, and those that are within the bounds of reasonable variations of human functions and structures. Of course, at the moment it is unclear how such distinctions can be made and morally justified. But the acknowledgement that it will be an extremely difficult task should not lead to the conclusion that it is impossible. Right here is a major challenge to philosophical reflection. Many moral discussions about whether or not to apply genetic knowledge seem essentially to focus on this issue in particular (for example, the debate on the development and use of human growth hormone; Wilkie, 1993).

The second factor is the normativity of medicine. Medicine regards itself ultimately as a helping and caring profession, not merely as a service institution. In such a self-conception, value-neutrality is not an appropriate position to guide medical activities. Physicians in this view adhere to professional norms that go beyond value neutrality. Diagnosis, therapy and prevention are guided and motivated by specific values, *viz* the promotion of health, relief of suffering, elimination of disease. From this value perspective, respect for individual autonomy is only an instrumental value, necessary in order to accomplish the values intrinsic to medicine as a helping and caring profession. The norm of non-directiveness in clinical human genetics, therefore, is inadequate from a medical point of view. It may have been prudent to introduce this norm against the background of historical misuse of genetic information. It may be desirable as a practical norm as long as genetic information is mainly related to genetic risks to the offspring. But it can be argued that in the present situation, where genetic testing is more and more concerned with detecting genetic risks for the future health of the individual person who is tested, the normative attitude of clinical geneticists should shift from neutrality to prescriptivity (De Wert, 1994). A similar point is made by Caplan: it is likely that a shift will occur from a normative stance of value neutrality toward 'an ethic in which the promotion of genetic health and the amelioration, prevention, and correction of genetic disease are the foundation of clinical and public health practice' (Caplan, 1992, p. 134). Decisions made on the basis of genetic information, should in this view aim at promoting health and alleviating disease. There is no reason to think that advocating these values in the realm of human genetics is inappropriate or unethical. Studies of the practice of clinical human genetics in fact indicate that those professionals who now offer genetic screening and testing services do not always act in conformity with their self-imposed ideal of value neutrality (Fletcher and Wertz, 1988).

Conclusion

In post-modern society two determinants are at work that will probably lead to a future where individual existence is to a large extent affected and permeated with predictive genetic information. First, we witness the current domination of the moral principle of respect for personal autonomy; the individual ought to choose from among the possible genetic tests those which fit his or her life plan. Second, society is moralising individual responsibility in the sense that persons who do not use the opportunities to foresee and prevent future suffering, have to face the consequences. Both factors give a strong push to know as much as possible about our life in the near and distant future. In this perspective the collective destiny of human beings in western societies will be deeply geneticized.

However, there are reasons to question the prediction of further geneticization. First, a clear opposition exists between the above determinants; the first emphasises the interest of the individual, the second the community interest. It is not evident which interest will prevail; it is not obvious that one interest will definitely overrule the other.

Second, autonomous individuals will not at random use everything available; they will sooner or later start to wonder what may be the meaning and relevance of all knowledge which is available and obtainable. Even within a fully free health market, individuals will not consume everything; they will attempt to make a distinction between appropriate and inappropriate, intelligible and unintelligible uses of genetic tests. This will instigate a public debate concerning the significance of genetic testing and genetic information, the more so since powerful parties such as insurance companies have an obvious interest in promoting testing. Third, it is doubtful whether future medicine will depart so radically from its present-day value orientation, especially in the European setting. The autonomous request of individual patients will be a significant moral factor, but, at the same time, medicine will also want to be guided by its own norms to make distinctions between disease and health, normality and abnormality. Beyond the individual demands and subjective complaints, medicine will continue to strive for a more rather than less objective determination of needs, signs and symptoms.

Apparently, a full geneticization of human existence in the future may only occur when we abandon the philosophical attempt to differentiate between 'healthy' and 'ill', 'normal' and 'abnormal'.

References

Caplan, A.L. (1992), *If I Were a Rich Man Could I Buy a Pancreas? and Other Essays on the Ethics of Health Care*, Indiana University Press: Bloomington and Indianapolis.

Collins, F.S. (1991), 'Medical and Ethical Consequences of the Human Genome Project', *The Journal of Clinical Ethics*, Vol. 2, No. 4, pp. 260-267.

De Wert, G. (1994), 'De oorlog tegen kanker, de jacht op kankergenen, en de speurtocht naar de ethiek', *Tijdschrift Kanker*, Vol. 18, No. 2, pp. 41-55.

Fletcher, J. and Wertz, D. (1988), *Ethics and Applied Human Genetics: A Cross-Cultural Perspective*, Springer Verlag: Heidelberg.

Fogle, T. (1995), 'Information Metaphors and the Human Genome Project', *Perspectives in Biology and Medicine*, Vol. 38, No. 4, pp. 535-547.

Hilhorst, M.T. (1993), 'Aangeboren en aangedane handicaps: maakt het moreel verschil?', in De Beaufort, I.D. and Hilhorst, M.T. (eds), *Kind, ziekte en ethiek*, pp. 67-91, Ambo: Baarn.

Lippman, A. (1992), 'Led (astray) by Genetic Maps: The Cartography of the Human Genome and Health Care', *Social Science and Medicine*, Vol. 35, No. 12, pp. 1469-1476.

Lupton, D. (1994), *Medicine as Culture. Illness, Disease and the Body in Western Societies*, Sage Publications: London.

Nelkin, D. and Lindee, M.S. (1995), *The DNA Mystique. The Gene as a Cultural Icon*, W.H. Freeman and Company: New York.

Ten Have, H.A.M.J. (1990), 'Knowledge and Practice in European Medicine: The Case of Infectious Diseases', in Ten Have, H.A.M.J., Kimsma, G.K. and Spicker, S.F. (eds), *The Growth of Medical Knowledge*, pp. 15-40, Kluwer Academic Publishers: Dordrecht, Boston, London.

Ten Have, H.A.M.J. and Loughlin, M. (1994), 'Responsibilities and Rationalities: Should the Patient be Blamed?', *Health Care Analysis*, Vol. 2, No. 2, pp. 119-127.

Watson, J.D. (1990), 'The Human Genome Project: Past, Present, and Future', *Science,* Vol. 248, pp. 44-48.

Wilkie, T. (1993), *Perilous Knowledge. The Human Genome Project and its Implications*, Faber and Faber: London, Boston.

Appendix 1 - The Euroscreen Project

Genetic screening: ethical and philosophical perspectives, with special reference to multifactorial diseases

The objectives of the Euroscreen project were to ascertain the extent of development of screening programmes in different European countries, to analyse the public policy responses to these developments and to make recommendations. Although primarily philosophical, the project has been interdisciplinary, with participants drawn from public health medicine, genetics, anthropology, law, history of medicine and sociology as well as philosophy. There were 25 participants from 16 European countries. The work of the project was co-ordinated by Professor Ruth Chadwick from the Centre for Professional Ethics, University of Central Lancashire.

The core group identified issues arising from different kinds of screening, used philosophical methods to clarify key concepts and developed a normative framework for approaching the issues.

In addition to the core group there were four sub-groups which considered the following;

1 Childhood testing for adult diseases

2 Concepts of health, disease and genetic predisposition.

3 Anthropological approaches.

4 Historical approaches

In 1996 the Euroscreen group was awarded a further research grant for three years to explore genetic information and insurance; commercialisation and genetic testing; and promoting public awareness. The project will be known as Euroscreen 2.

Name	University/Institute	Country
Core Group Members		
Ruth Chadwick	University of Central Lancashire, Preston	United Kingdom
Henk ten Have	Katholieke Universiteit Nijmegen	The Netherlands
Jørgen Husted	Aarhus University	Denmark
Mairi Levitt	University of Central Lancashire, Preston	United Kingdom
Tony McGleenan	Queen's University of Belfast	United Kingdom
Darren Shickle	University of Wales, College of Medicine, Cardiff	United Kingdom
Urban Wiesing	Westfälische Wilhelms-Universität Münster	Germany
Euroscreen Administrator		
Kerry Wilding	University of Central Lancashire, Preston	United Kingdom
Co-ordinators of a Sub-Group		
Brunetto Chiarelli	University of Florence	Italy
Angus Clarke	University of Wales, College of Medicine, Cardiff	United Kingdom
Ingmar Pörn	University of Helsinki	Finland
Urban Wiesing	Westfälische Wilhelms-Universität Münster	Germany
Participants		
Andrew Belsey	University of Wales College of Cardiff	United Kingdom
André Boué	Comité Consultatif National d'Ethique pour les Sciences de la Vie et de la Santé, Paris	France
Kris Dierickx	Katholieke Universiteit Leuven	Belgium
Vladimir Ferak	Comenius University, Bratislava	Slovakia
Gertrud Hauser	University of Vienna	Austria
Rogeer Hoedemaekers	Katholieke Universiteit Nijmegen	The Netherlands
Hans-Peter Kröner	Westfälische Wilhelms-Universität Münster	Germany
Veikko Launis	University of Turku	Finland
Judit Sandor	Central European University, Budapest	Hungary
Jirí Šantavý	Palacký University, Olomouc	Czech Republic
Traute Schröder-Kurth	Eibelstadt	Germany
Luca Sineo	University of Florence	Italy
Consultants		
Richard Benson, CM	Archdiocese of Los Angeles	USA
Dolores Dooley	University College Cork	Ireland
M.L. Rodrigues de Areia	University of Coimbra	Portugal

Appendix 2 - Glossary

This glossary does not provide a comprehensive list of genetic disorders. Only those terms used in the text are included and definitions are simply intended to aid the general reader.

Adrendeukodystrophy (ALD)   A rare disorder affecting boys and inherited through the mother who carries the defective gene on an X chromosome. Boys have a 50 per cent risk of inheriting the disease and girls have a 50 per cent chance of being carriers. The disease affects the adrenal glands and boys usually die in childhood.

Alzheimer's disease A degenerative disorder causing dementia with onset in middle to old age. The gene *ApoE* has been implicated in the disease.

Autosomal disorders carried on one of the 22 matched pairs of chromosomes (one from each parent) which are not involved in sex determination.

BRCA1 gene (and BRCA2 gene) the so-called breast cancer genes thought to be linked to 5 per cent of breast cancer cases. Those carrying one of the genes have an 85% of developing breast cancer.

Cystic fibrosis An inherited recessive disease affecting the lungs and digestive system. Couples who are both healthy carriers have a one in four chance of having an affected child at each pregnancy. More prevalent among Caucasians.

Dominant disorder   A genetic disorder apparent when only one of the two copies of the gene is defective (i.e. the gene only needs to be inherited from one parent) e.g. Huntington's disease.

Down's syndrome A genetic anomaly which is not usually inherited. Affected individuals are mentally handicapped and have a reduced life expectancy. The incidence rises with maternal age. Genetic screening and termination of affected fetuses is routinely offered to expectant 'older' mothers in most European countries (the exact age group varies).

Fragile X The most common form of inherited mental retardation caused by a mutation on the X chromosome. All boys with the mutation are affected but some girls have only mild learning difficulties or no symptoms at all. Genetic testing is possible.

Genotype An individual's genetic make-up.

Huntington's disease (Huntington's chorea) An autosomal dominant disease causing progressive degeneration of the central nervous system. Onset is generally in middle age. One affected parent has a 50 per cent chance of having an affected child at each pregnancy.

Multifactorial disease Disease associated with a number of factors e.g. environmental, genetic and social.

PKU (Phenylketonuria) A rare disorder which causes severe mental retardation unless babies are put on a special diet. Neonatal screening (by blood test) is routine in most European countries and USA.

Polycystic kidney disease An inherited disease in which the kidneys contain many cysts. The adult (autosomal dominant) type leads to renal failure around the age of 50. Can be detected by prenatal testing.

Population screening A programme offering screening to groups of asymptomatic individuals rather than to those with symptoms or with family members having the disorder. May be used to identify those who will be offered further testing e.g. pregnant women found to be carriers of a genetic disorder would be offered prenatal diagnosis.

Preimplantation screening Screening of the embryo before placing in the womb made possible through the use of in vitro fertilisation technology (IVF) e.g. screening for a genetic disorder. Illegal in Germany since 1990.

Recessive disorder A genetic disorder apparent only if copies of the defective gene are inherited from both parents e.g. cystic fibrosis.

Serum screening test Screening a maternal blood sample e.g. for abnormal levels of alpha-fetoprotein which might indicate certain malformations of the fetus (serum is the fluid in blood plasma).

Sickle cell disease A group of inherited disorders of the haemoglobin. Red blood cells become sickle shaped causing blockage of blood vessels and pain and damage to organs. Mainly found among those of African and Caribbean descent. Mass screening (compulsory in some instances) was at first welcomed by African-Americans in the early 1970's but resulted in discrimination against healthy carriers and fuelled racial prejudice.

Tay-sachs A recessive disorder found mainly among Ashkenazi Jewish families. Causes deterioration of the brain and muscle function with death usually occurring in infancy. Voluntary screening programmes have been seen as successful in the USA - carrier couples avoid marrying (where marriages are arranged) or have prenatal screening. However, only a minority of the Ashkenazi Jewish population take up screening even in the USA.

Thalassemia A genetic recessive disorder of the haemoglobin which causes severe anaemia. Children with thalassemia major usually die by the age of ten if it is untreated. The disease is widely spread among the Mediterranean population with a high incidence in Cyprus where one in seven of the population are carriers. The incidence of affected births has been reduced by nearly 98 per cent in Cyprus through testing before marriage and the use of prenatal diagnosis by carrier couples and termination of affected fetuses. The Orthodox Church requires a premarital certificate stating the person has been tested before the marriage will be blessed.

X linked Form of inheritance where the gene is carried on the X chromosome.

Jesus and Me

Bible Storybook

Jesus and Me
Bible Storybook

by Stephen Elkins

illustrated by
Claudine Gévry

A Division of Thomas Nelson Publishers

NASHVILLE   DALLAS   MEXICO CITY   RIO DE JANEIRO

Published in Nashville, Tennessee, by Tommy Nelson. Tommy Nelson is an imprint of Thomas Nelson. Thomas Nelson is a registered trademark of HarperCollins Christian Publishing, Inc.

ALL NEW MATERIAL
Filling: Polyurethane Foam
REG. No. PA-14954 (CN), MA-3031 (CN)
Made in China
TSSA Reg. No 07T-00912512

Unless otherwise noted, Scripture quotations are taken from the International Children's Bible®. © 1986, 1988, 1999 by Thomas Nelson. All rights reserved.

ISBN 13: 978-1-4003-2369-2

Printed in China

14 15 16 17 DSC 6 5 4 3 2 1

Contents

· · · · · · · · · · · ·

Jesus

"For God loved the world so much that
he gave his only Son. God gave his
Son so that whoever believes in him may
not be lost, but have eternal life."
—John 3:16

Dear Parents,

Jesus and Me Bible Storybook was written to help teach children about the life of Christ and how to enter a lifelong relationship with Him. For the purpose of this book, the stories are written in past tense, as they refer to specific events that happened when Jesus was walking on the earth. However, we are blessed to serve a risen Savior who holds the same power today to heal, bless, and forgive as He did two thousand years ago.

I hope you and your children enjoy this book and are blessed by His presence.

Sincerely,
Stephen Elkins

When Did Moses Speak About Jesus?

Deuteronomy 18:15; John 1:45; 5:45–46; Luke 24:27

J esus was the **Son of God**. But the Jews wanted proof. According to the Law of Moses, Jesus needed a witness to speak on His behalf. So Jesus told the Jews that Moses had written about Him. Fourteen hundred years before Jesus was born, Moses wrote, "The Lord your God will give you a prophet like me. He will be one of your own people. Listen to him."

How was Jesus like Moses? They were both prophets, priests, lawgivers, and leaders of men. They both taught new truths and new commandments. And they both performed miracles. After Philip met Jesus, he found Nathanael and told him, "Remember that Moses wrote in the law about a man who was coming. . . . We have found him. He is Jesus."

Dear Father, thank You for Jesus! Because those who find Him find peace. Amen.

Jesus and Me . . .

There's another way Jesus was like Moses. Moses was called a deliverer. He obeyed God and delivered the Israelites from captivity in Egypt. Jesus was called "Deliverer" too. He delivers you and me from another kind of captivity—that of sin and death. That is why it is so important to find Jesus! Ask Him into your heart today!

Prophets Said Jesus Was the Promised One

Isaiah 9:6; Micah 5:2; Zechariah 12:10; Psalm 22:16–18

Dear Father, I believe the promise. I believe that Jesus is coming again. Help me share that good news with others. Amen.

Prophets were messengers for God. They told about things that would happen in the future. Isaiah was one of the greatest prophets. He lived eight hundred years before Jesus was born. But listen to the words Isaiah wrote about Jesus: "A child will be born to us. God will give a son to us. . . . His name will be Wonderful Counselor, Powerful God, Father Who Lives Forever, Prince of Peace."

Through Isaiah, God gave us the wonderful promise of Jesus. But Isaiah wasn't the only prophet who spoke about Jesus. Micah told where He would be born; Zechariah said His side would be pierced; David said He would be crucified.

And they all said that someday the **Promised One** would come!

Jesus and Me . . .

Jesus gave us another promise before leaving the earth and returning to heaven. Did you know that Jesus promised to come **a second time**? When He came the first time, not everyone got to see Him. But when He comes again, every eye will see Him coming in the clouds!

John the Disciple Said Jesus Was the Word

. . . .

John 1:1; 14:9; Luke 13:3

The very first verse in the book of John tells us who Jesus is. John calls Him "**the Word**." Words help us understand things. Words describe things others have not seen, and words can save us from dangerous situations. For example, we shout, "Stop!" to prevent an accident.

John calls Jesus "the Word" because it is Jesus who helps us understand who God is. We haven't seen God, but Jesus tells us about God when He says, "He who has seen me has seen the Father." It is Jesus who tells us about heaven, and it is Jesus who saves us from the dangers of sin. "Change your hearts and lives!" He warns.

Jesus is the walking, talking, living, breathing Word of God.

Dear Father, thank You for Jesus, Your Word made flesh. And thank You for the Bible, Your Word made paper! Amen.

Jesus and Me . . .

Jesus is the Word of God **made flesh**. He was sent to accomplish God's plan. What was God's plan? To save you and me from sin! God's Word was "made flesh" in Jesus. God's Word has also been "made paper." It's called the Bible! Read it every day.

The Angel Said Jesus Was the Son of God

Luke 1:26–38

More than three hundred prophecies had been written about the coming Messiah. Jesus was coming soon! And God's very special plan would include a young Jewish girl named Mary. God sent the angel Gabriel to visit Mary.

Seeing an angel might frighten anyone! So Gabriel said, "Don't be afraid, Mary, because God is pleased with you. Listen! . . . You will give birth to a son, and you will name him Jesus. . . . He will be called the **Son of God**."

Mary trusted God and she said, "Let this happen to me as you say!" Then the angel went away as quickly as he had appeared.

Lord, I have been given a measure of faith.
Help it to grow more and more each day. Amen.

Jesus and Me . . .

God was pleased with Mary. What was it about Mary that pleased God so much? The Bible says, "Without faith no one can please God." Faith is believing that God will do what He promises. Mary **believed** God's promises. How is your faith right now? Are you trusting God day by day? Can you say, like Mary, "Do what You will, Lord"? Pleasing God always begins with faith!

A Special Name for
a Special Baby

. . . .

Luke 1:30–31; Matthew 1:20–21

When God makes a plan, no detail is left out. So when He planned to send a Savior into this world, He had just the right name picked out. What was it?

When the angel Gabriel first appeared to Mary, he told her, "You will give birth to a son, and you will name him Jesus." Later an angel also appeared to Joseph in a dream. The angel said to Joseph, "Mary will give birth to a son. You will name the son Jesus. Give him that name because he will save his people from their sins."

The name **Jesus** is Greek for the Hebrew name *Yeshua*, which means "God saves." What the angel said to Joseph was this: call His name "God saves" because He will save His people from their sins.

So Mary and Joseph obeyed the command of God. They named this Child—who had been sent from God—Jesus.

Dear Father, thank You for Jesus. Thank You that He has saved me. I want my family and friends to be saved too. May they come to know Jesus soon! Amen.

Jesus and Me . . .

Jesus was sent to save. Are you saved? What does it mean to **be saved**? Being saved means that you are rescued from danger. Jesus rescues us from the danger of missing heaven and being separated from God forever. Jesus is the One who rescues and saves us from the penalties of sin!

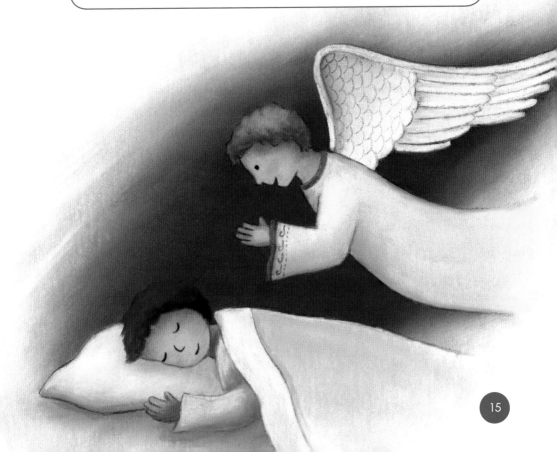

15

When Was Jesus Born?

Galatians 4:4

God's timing is always perfect. He is never too early or too late. He is never in a hurry and—unlike you and me—He is always on time. The Bible says that "when the right time came, God sent his Son." Through the ages, God had been preparing the world for the coming of Jesus.

Many prophets had told about Jesus' coming, and the Jewish people were watching for the promised **Messiah**. The world was united under Roman rule, and the Romans had built good roads to every part of the world. Greek was a common language. All of this was just perfect for spreading Jesus' message of hope to people everywhere!

Jesus was indeed born at just the right time!

Dear Father, I am Your creation. You've made me special to do special things. Help me do the things You want me to do. Amen.

Jesus and Me . . .

Ever wonder why you weren't born a hundred years ago or even a thousand years ago? You were born at just the **right time**, with just the right talents and skills to do the job God prepared for you to do. You are not here by chance. God has a very special purpose for your life! So keep your eyes and ears open. Listen for His still, small voice!

17

Where Was Jesus Born?

Luke 2:1–7; Micah 5:2–5

Caesar Augustus wanted to know how many people lived in his kingdom. So he commanded everyone to return to their hometown to be counted. Joseph and Mary were among those making the journey from Nazareth to the town of Bethlehem.

Bethlehem was called the City of David. And since Joseph was related to King David, Bethlehem was considered Joseph's hometown. They traveled through several villages and five miles past Jerusalem to the little town of Bethlehem, where Jesus was born.

Many years before, the prophet Micah had said that a ruler would come out of Bethlehem who would take care of His people. Jesus was that great ruler!

Dear Father, I know You have placed me where I am for a reason. Help me, Lord, to always do Your will. Amen.

Jesus and Me . . .

Not only were you born at just the right time; you were also born in just the **right place**. God has placed you where you are to do a work just for Him. There may be friends in your hometown who need to hear about God's love. There may be family members you can tell about Jesus. God is like a gardener. He plants us right where He wants us to grow . . . and we grow in grace!

The Wise Men Said Jesus Was the King of the Jews

Matthew 2:1–12

After the birth of Jesus, magi, or wise men from eastern countries, made their way to Jerusalem to find the King of kings. God sent a bright star to lead them to Jesus. When they arrived in Jerusalem, they asked, "Where is the baby who was born to be the **king of the Jews**? . . . We came to worship him."

Upon seeing Jesus, they knelt down and worshipped Him. And they offered Him these gifts: gold, which was a fitting gift for a king; frankincense, which was a healing medicine; and myrrh, which was a perfume used in burials.

Such perfect gifts for the King who would *heal* His people and then one day *die* on a cross to save them.

Dear Father, show me the things that have eternal value so that my treasure is stored up in heaven! Amen.

Have you ever wondered why the King of kings had no royal bed, but just a feeding box? Or why the **Lord of lords** slept among peasants and not in a palace? Maybe God was changing attitudes that night. That little manger said to the world: *The things of earth are not important. Seek heavenly treasure, not the comforts of earth!*

Where Did Jesus Teach as a Boy?

Luke 2:41–52

When Jesus was twelve years old, Mary and Joseph took Him to Jerusalem to celebrate the Passover. They stayed for several days. At that time, it was common for large groups of families to travel together. So as Mary and Joseph headed home, they thought Jesus was with their group. When they couldn't find Him, they hurried back to Jerusalem. After three days, they found Him **in the temple**, where the teachers were amazed at His knowledge.

When Mary told Jesus they had been worried, Jesus answered, "You should have known that I must be where my Father's work is!" Jesus returned to Nazareth, where He continued to learn more and to grow.

As Jesus grew up, people liked Him and God was pleased with Him.

Dear Father, I know You are working everywhere—even through children! Give me the courage to tell someone this week about Your awesome love! Amen.

Jesus and Me . . .

Jesus wanted to be where God was working. So we ask ourselves, *Where is God working today?* He is working **everywhere**! He is working in your family. He is working in your church. He works in schools and even on playgrounds. Wherever the message of God's love can be shared, that is the place where God is working.

Where Did Jesus Grow Up?

Mark 1:9; Luke 1:26–27; John 1:45–46

Nazareth was a small town in the north of Israel, settled in a valley with hills all around it. It was there that the angel Gabriel visited Mary to tell her that she would be the mother of Jesus. He was known to many as Jesus the Nazarene because **Nazareth** was His childhood home. When Philip told Nathanael that Jesus was from Nazareth, he remarked, "Nazareth! Can anything good come from Nazareth?"

But we know that something good did come from Nazareth: salvation through our Lord Jesus Christ. In fact, it's better than good! Salvation is the greatest gift of all!

Dear Father, help me to be more like Jesus and to do good work for You. Amen.

Jesus and Me . . .

What's the name of the city or town you live in? Is it a nice town? I'm sure it is. And just like Nazareth, something good can come out of your town too. Do you know what it is? **YOU**! The Bible says we're all created in Christ Jesus to do good works. So no matter what town you live in, something good can come out of it. Just keep following Jesus!

When Did Jesus' Ministry Begin?

Matthew 3:13–17; Acts 2

T he word *ministry* means "to serve." Jesus' ministry began at the Jordan River, right after He was baptized. As He came up out of the water, heaven opened and **God's Spirit** came down on Him like a dove. At that moment, His earthly ministry began.

And the same thing happened to the disciples and to the first Christian church after Jesus went back to heaven. God's Spirit came down on a day called Pentecost, when three thousand people were saved!

Jesus' ministry began when God's Spirit came to Him, and ours does too.

Dear Father, I want to serve You. Help me discover the plans You have for me! Amen.

Have you ever wondered what ministry God has planned for you? Will you go to some faraway land and teach about **God's love**? Or will you serve the Lord in your community or home? One thing's for sure: God has a place for everyone to serve Him. He has a place for you!

John the Baptist Said Jesus Was the Lamb of God

Matthew 3:1–6; John 1:28–31

He wore clothes made of camel hair. He ate locusts and wild honey and lived in the desert. He was John the Baptist. And it was John's job to prepare the people for the coming of Jesus.

One day, as John stood baptizing sinners in the Jordan River, he saw Jesus walking down the hillside toward him. John said, "Look, the **Lamb of God**. He takes away the sins of the world!" John called Jesus the Lamb of God because—like the lambs that were sacrificed in the Old Testament times—Jesus would be offered as a sacrifice to save His people.

Dear Father, please help me to tell someone this week about Jesus, who is coming back soon. Amen.

John the Baptist was **preparing** people for the coming of Jesus. That's what we should do too! We must tell our family and friends that Jesus is coming back soon. We don't want them to be surprised and unprepared. Let's all be like John the Baptist and tell everyone about our coming Savior. But please . . . don't eat any locusts!

He Taught About Baptism

Matthew 3

When Jesus was a little boy, the Greeks had a word they used on laundry days. The word was *bapto,* which was when a piece of clothing was dipped in bleach and then into a dye. The bleach cleaned the cloth, and then the dye gave it a new color.

The word *baptism* comes from the Greek word *bapto.* Baptism is an outward sign that we have been cleansed and changed on the inside. We have been cleansed from sin and changed because we have asked Jesus into our hearts.

Because of Jesus, all our sins have been washed away.

Dear Father, when the time is right, I want to be baptized, just like Jesus! Help me know when that day is here. Amen.

Jesus and Me . . .

When you ask Jesus into your heart, something amazing happens. It's like that piece of dirty cloth on laundry day. You are **changed** forever! All the sin in your life is washed away, like dirty water going down the drain. And you are changed! That's because Jesus is now living in your heart. When this happens, you may want to be baptized. That tells the world that Jesus has cleaned you and changed you!

Where Was Jesus Baptized?

Matthew 3:13–17

I t starts where two rivers from Lebanon and Syria meet. Its waters flow 156 miles through the valleys and plains of Israel into the Sea of Galilee. On it goes to the south, where it ends at the Dead Sea. It's called the Jordan River. It is the largest and longest river in Israel and the only river in Israel that is never dry.

The Bible says Jesus came to the Jordan River to be **baptized** by John. John said, "I should be baptized by you!"

But Jesus answered, "Let it be this way for now. We should do all things that are right."

So there in the Jordan River, close to where its waters enter the Sea of Galilee, Jesus was baptized.

Dear Father, help me to love Jesus and to trust Him with my life. And when the time is right, may I follow Him in obedience and be baptized. Amen.

Some are baptized in a river or lake. Others choose to be baptized in a church or even a swimming pool. The place is not really important. But our obedience is. We are baptized in **obedience** to the Scriptures. When you do this, you let the world know that you love Jesus and that you trust Him with your life!

God the Father Said Jesus Was His Beloved Son

. . . .

Mark 1:9–11

Don't you just love it when your father is pleased with you? There's joy that comes with hearing the words, "I'm proud of you!" Did you know that Jesus' Father was pleased with Him? When Jesus came to John the Baptist to be baptized, John was confused. He knew that Jesus always did what was right and had no need for baptism.

But Jesus assured John that it was the right thing to do. And as Jesus came up out of the water, a voice spoke from heaven. It was His Father's voice. And He said, "You are **my Son** and I love you. I am very pleased with you."

God is always pleased when we do His will.

Dear Father, I want my life to be pleasing to You. You are a wonderful God! Amen.

Jesus and Me . . .

Will God be pleased when you choose to be baptized? Of course He will! Nothing pleases God more than a loving heart lifted in praise to Him. And that is what baptism really is. It says, "I love You, Lord! I love You enough to trust You with my life." That kind of **faith** pleases God more than anything. And He will be very pleased with you too!

Where Was Jesus Tempted by the Devil?

Matthew 4:1–11

God the Father was pleased as Jesus' ministry began. But the Devil was not! Jesus went into the **wilderness** to fast and pray; the Devil waited for his chance to tempt Him. The wilderness of Judea was an area close to the Dead Sea. It is very dry and rocky.

After Jesus had fasted for forty days, the Devil appeared to Him. He tempted our Lord in every way possible. But Jesus answered each temptation by quoting the Word of God. "Go away from me, Satan!" said Jesus. "It is written in the Scriptures, 'You must worship the Lord your God. Serve only him!'"

That's how you defeat the Devil. When the Devil is heard, just speak the Word of God!

Dear Father, when I am tempted to do bad things, help me do what Jesus did. May I answer that temptation with a Bible verse. Amen.

Everyone who loves the Lord must be prepared for temptation. How do we **prepare**? We do what Jesus did. Answer temptation with a Bible verse. Are you tempted to say bad things? Think about what the Bible teaches: "Let no bad words come out of my mouth." Are you tempted to lie? Quote Scripture: "Speak the truth with love." Jesus showed us how to overcome temptation: quote Bible verses!

He Taught About Repentance

Matthew 4:17

Jesus tells us to *repent*, which means to change our hearts and minds for God. Jesus said, "Change your hearts and lives because the kingdom of heaven is coming soon."

When we repent, we do two very important things: First, we change our hearts. That changes how we think. We come to see that our way of doing things is not like God's way. And second, we change what we do. Instead of doing the things that please us, we choose to do the things that please God. To repent means we **change our hearts**, and we change our lives. We turn away from sin and turn toward God.

Repent! Now, that's a real change.

Dear Father, I know that real repentance means real change. Help me think about You and act in a way that is pleasing to You. Amen.

Jesus and Me . . .

Changing how we think and how we act can be hard. But remember, you're not alone! Jesus knows how hard it is. With His help, you can replace those bad habits with **good habits** that please God. Turn away from sin, and turn toward God. Now, that's repentance!

Where Did Jesus Call Many of His Disciples?

Mark 1:16–20; Luke 5:27–28; Luke 6:13–16; Acts 1:13

There is a body of water in Israel called the **Sea of Galilee**. It is a place Jesus knew well. He walked on its stormy waters. He spoke to its waves, and they were quieted. Once, He met several fishermen on its shore. "Come and follow me," Jesus said. Peter and Andrew followed. Later He called James and John, and they followed Him too. Jesus had twelve disciples.

Where did the other disciples who followed Jesus come from? Six more also came from the area of Galilee: Philip and his friend Nathanael; Thomas, known as doubting Thomas; James, the son of Alpheus; Judas, son of James; and Simon the Zealot. Matthew, the tax collector, came from Capernaum. Judas Iscariot, the one who betrayed Jesus, came from Judea.

Dear Father, make me a better fisherman for Jesus. Help me show kindness to all and show them the love You have for all people! Amen.

Jesus wants us to be disciples, just like Peter, James, and John. He wants us to **follow Him** and be like Him! And what does that mean? We fish! We fish for people, which means we catch them with our kindness and lead them into the kingdom of God!

How Does Jesus Want Us to Live?

Matthew 5:13–16; 1 Corinthians 7:31

The greatest sermon ever preached happened on a mountain-side near Jerusalem. It was there that Jesus explained how He wants us to live. "You are the salt of the earth," He said. "You are to shine like a light in the world."

What in the world did Jesus mean by that? It's hard to imagine a time when there were no refrigerators. But in Jesus' time, salt was used to keep food fresh. People would rub salt into their food to save and preserve it.

Likewise, the apostle Paul said that this world "will soon be gone," kind of like food that's not refrigerated. So we are to be like salt, "rubbing in" the gospel of Jesus to everyone we meet! We should tell people about Jesus, about how He preserves and saves!

Jesus also said we are to be a "light to the world." Light helps people see; it illuminates the path and chases away the darkness. We are to live our lives as a light to guide others to Jesus.

Dear Lord, help me to be salt and light to those I meet every day. May I be the one to show them the love of God and tell them about Jesus! Amen.

Jesus and Me . . .

How can we be salt and light in the world today? Live for Jesus! Believe in your heart that Jesus is the way to heaven. And "declare with your mouth" too. If we're **salty**, we'll make people **thirsty** for Jesus. If we are **light**, we'll help people **see** God's plan. Be salt and light to those around you!

He Taught Us to Pray

Matthew 6:5–13

God wants to talk to you! But how? Through prayer!

Jesus taught us how to pray. First, we should **praise** God: *"Our Father in heaven, we pray that Your name will always be kept holy."* Then we should **ask** God to help us do what He wants us to do: *"We pray that Your kingdom will come. We pray that what You want will be done, here on earth as it is in heaven."*

Jesus said we should then ask God for the things we need: *"Give us the food we need for each day."* We should also **confess** our sins: *"Forgive the sins we have done, just as we have forgiven those who did wrong to us."*

Finally, we should ask God to lead us every day and to keep us safe from the evil one: *"Do not cause us to be tested; but save us from the Evil One."*

Remember, God loves you, and He wants you to talk to Him every day!

Dear God, I am so glad You love to talk to kids. We love to talk to You too! Thank You for always being there. Amen.

Jesus and Me . . .

It is rather hard to imagine that the most powerful Person in the whole universe wants to talk to you! He wants to **talk** to you each and every day. He wants to share your joys and your troubles. And it's all because He made you and loves you so much. So pray and talk to your very best friend!

Where Can We Find God's Kingdom?

Matthew 6:10; Luke 17:20

Jesus prayed to God His Father. He prayed that God's kingdom would come. What did He mean?

A **kingdom** is a place where a king rules. And a kingdom must have people who are willing to obey and serve the king. God's kingdom is the place where God rules. So we find God's kingdom wherever we find people who honor Him as ruler of their lives.

Jesus said, "God's kingdom is coming, but not in a way that you will be able to see with your eyes." That's because God's kingdom is within us.

We find God's kingdom in the hearts of those who honor Him as king.

Dear Father, come live in my heart.
Make it Your kingdom. Live there and work
in me what is pleasing in Your sight. Amen.

Jesus and Me . . .

When Jesus comes into our **hearts**, His love and grace begin to flow out of us in word and deed. We seem different to others. That's because the King has come and changed everything. Now we serve Him and do all that we do for Him! God's kingdom is a very special place. And that place is your heart!

He Taught the Golden Rule

Matthew 7:12

Which would you want: a truckload of pennies or a couple of gold bricks? Gold bricks? Good choice! Gold is very valuable, and that's why the **"Golden Rule"** is called golden! It teaches us a lesson of great value: "Do for other people the same things you want them to do for you."

Jesus was saying we should treat others as we would like to be treated. Would you like someone to cut in front of you in line or take the toys you are using? No! Treat others the way you want to be treated! It's easy to say but a little harder to do. But once you get the hang of it, the Golden Rule can make you rich in love!

Treating others well pleases Jesus!

Lord, may I be golden every day. And forgive me when I'm not so golden. Help me to value all people as I do myself. Amen.

But what about all those times when you aren't so "golden"? Maybe you were selfish and didn't treat others the way you want to be treated. Ask God to forgive you. He will be **pleased** that you want to do better. The Golden Rule isn't always easy to do, but practice makes perfect! Be "golden" every day!

When Did Nicodemus Come to Jesus?

John 3:1–21

Nicodemus was a wise ruler of the Jewish temple. He wanted to know more about Jesus, so he arranged to meet Jesus **at night**. "We know that you are a teacher sent from God," Nicodemus said.

Jesus answered him in a curious way: "I tell you the truth. Unless you are born again, you cannot be in God's kingdom."

Puzzled, Nicodemus asked, "But if a man is already old, how can he be born again?"

When a baby is born, he leaves the darkness of his mother's womb and comes out into the light. Jesus was telling Nicodemus that to be in God's kingdom, you must come out of this dark world and be born into the light of God's kingdom.

Dear Father, I come to You right now. Come into my heart and be my Savior. Amen.

Nicodemus came to Jesus at night. Some come to Jesus in the morning, some at noon or evening time. It really doesn't matter what time you come, as long as you come! He is always there with outstretched arms, ready to **welcome** you into the kingdom of God. Don't wait a minute longer! Right now is the perfect time to invite Jesus into your heart.

How Long Does Salvation Last?

John 3:16

Salvation is everlasting! If you had a pair of everlasting shoes, they would *never* wear out. If you had an everlasting gallon of milk, it would *never* be empty. And if you had **everlasting** energy, on and on you'd go, and you would never, ever stop.

On earth, we all run out of steam eventually. But God has promised everlasting life to those who accept Jesus as their Savior. That means that no matter how long you may live with Jesus in heaven, there is always one more day to live. In this world, we are born and then someday we die. But when we are saved, John 3:16 says we receive everlasting life.

So how long does salvation last? Always one more day!

Dear Father, I come to You for salvation. I know that because of Jesus, I am saved from Your judgment and saved to Your heaven forever. Thank You, Lord, for Your wonderful saving grace! Amen.

It is the most amazing gift anyone could ever receive. It doesn't cost anything, and yet it's priceless! You can't earn it. It can only be given to you. It lasts forever, it's called **salvation**, and it's a double blessing! Jesus has saved us *from* the judgment of God. And we are saved *to* an eternity with Him in heaven! Salvation is an amazing gift given to you by God!

How Do We Receive Eternal Life?

John 3:16; 5:24

Birthdays are so much fun! And the best part of a birthday is opening the gifts! A *gift* is something you receive from someone who cares about you. You don't have to pay for it. It's given freely. Someone else bought the gift and delivered it to you with a big, bright bow.

The Bible says that God has given us a gift too! It is the gift of eternal life through Jesus Christ. When Jesus died on the cross, He paid for that gift. He paid with His life because He cared so much. The gift He gave was eternal life. Because of His gift, we can live forever with Him in heaven. But you have to receive it. How? It's easy . . . just pray this prayer:

Dear God, I believe that Jesus is Your Son. I know He is a gift You have given to me. Because of Jesus, I now have eternal life. By faith, I believe that Jesus has paid for my gift with His life. I receive Your gift. I receive Jesus. Amen.

We receive the gift of eternal life by accepting Jesus as our Savior.

Jesus and Me . . .

Some gifts last for just a little while, like an ice-cream cone. It doesn't last very long, does it? Other gifts last much longer, like a new bicycle. But one day that bicycle will get old and wear out. What God gives us is **eternal**. And eternal things last forever! When we receive God's gift of *eternal life*, we live forever with Jesus!

The Samaritans Said Jesus Was the Savior of the World

John 4:1–42

In the days of Jesus, Jews and Samaritans lived in the same region. But they didn't like each other. A Jewish person would not even talk to a Samaritan . . . but Jesus did.

One day, Jesus, who was a Jew, met a Samaritan woman at a well. Jesus said to her, "Please give me a drink."

The woman was surprised because Jesus spoke to her with kindness. As they began to talk, Jesus told the Samaritan woman many things about herself. The woman said, "I know that the Messiah is coming."

Then Jesus said, "He is talking to you now. I am he."

The Samaritan woman believed. She brought her friends to Jesus, and they believed too, saying, "This man really is **the Savior of the world**."

Dear Father, I want to be like the Samaritan woman by bringing my friends to Jesus! Amen.

The Samaritan woman set an example we should follow. After meeting Jesus and listening to Him, she **believed**! She believed He was indeed the Savior of the world, sent by God above. And she didn't keep what she had learned to herself. She called her friends and neighbors. She brought them to Jesus. And guess what? They believed in Jesus too! Just like the Samaritan woman, we should bring our friends to Jesus!

He Taught Using Parables

Matthew 7:24–27; 13:13, 31–32; 20:1–16; Luke 10:30–37; 15:1–10

All great teachers have one thing in common. They make their lessons easy to understand. That is why Jesus was the greatest teacher of all. He used simple parables to teach many of His greatest lessons.

Parables are **short stories** that use common, everyday things to teach about God's kingdom. Jesus used a mustard seed to teach about faith. Stories of lost sheep and coins were used to teach about God's forgiveness. He told stories about good neighbors and vineyards and building houses to teach us how to live godly lives.

Yes, Jesus used ordinary things to teach extraordinary lessons.

Dear Father, thank You that Jesus used easy-to-remember stories to teach us the lessons of heaven. Amen.

Do you have a favorite parable taught by Jesus? The story of the Good Samaritan is a favorite of many. When Jesus was asked to explain who His neighbor was, He answered with a **parable**. He told of a man who was hurt. A Samaritan stopped to help a total stranger. Jesus told the Pharisees to go and do the same thing. Everyone in need is your neighbor!

The Wise and Foolish Builders

Matthew 7:24–27

One day Jesus was teaching a great crowd. He compared a strong house to a strong life. Each must be anchored. Each must be built on something solid because storms will come.

Jesus said wise men build their house on a rock. Builders know that a rock is a **good foundation** because rocks are strong and do not move. So when the storms come, that house stands. But Jesus said foolish men build their houses on sand. Storms wash them away.

Building our lives on God's Word helps us to endure troubles that are sure to come. It's like building our lives on a strong rock!

Dear Father, I want to build my life on the Solid Rock. And I know that rock is the Bible. May I read Your Word every day! Amen.

Jesus and Me . . .

The Bible is the strong rock you and I should build on. We start out learning easy lessons. We learn about God's love and how we are to treat others. Then as we grow, our faith grows! We learn about God's **saving love** and the grace that will help us each and every day. Making good choices and decisions begins with an open Bible. That's building on God's Word—the Solid Rock!

The Sower and the Seeds

Matthew 13:3–8, 18–23

On another day, Jesus taught using the example of soil and seeds. He said seeds are like the Word of God, and our hearts are like soil. When we tell others about Jesus, it's like **planting seeds**!

Do all people say yes to Jesus? No! Some seeds fall on hard soil. Other seeds fall on good soil and grow a fruitful crop! This parable compared people's heart to different kinds of dirt! Some accept Jesus and others do not. Some are too troubled and worried to hear about the kingdom of heaven.

The important thing is to keep sowing the seed . . . keep telling others about Jesus!

Dear Father, I give all my troubles and worries to You right now. Help me to hear from You as I read Your Word and listen in prayer—and to share the good news of Jesus wherever I go. Amen.

How is your heart? Are you troubled about something? Has worry crept into your life? Remember, your heart is like soil. When you allow trouble and worry into your life, it's hard to hear from God. But when you **pray** and give all your troubles and worries to Jesus, it's easy to hear from God!

The Mustard Seed

Matthew 13:31–32

Jesus told many parables. In this one, Jesus compares the kingdom of heaven to a mustard seed. Mustard seeds are the **smallest** of all seeds. You can hardly see one in your hand! Yet when the mustard seed is planted in a garden, it becomes the **largest** of all the garden plants—so big, in fact, that the birds come and build their nests in the branches! Small seeds can grow into very large trees!

Dear Father, my faith is pretty small right now. I'm just a kid. But I know one day my faith will be big. Help my faith to grow! Amen.

Faith is like a mustard seed. It starts out very small. But as you walk with God day to day and see all the wonderful things He does, your faith grows. You see prayers answered. You see blessing after blessing. Your faith grows **bigger** and **stronger** until it is the biggest and most important part of your life!

The Pearl

. . . .

Matthew 13:44–46

Jesus told a parable about heaven. He told of a man who had an unusual job. This man searched the world as a buyer and seller of pearls. Pearls are very **valuable** and very **beautiful**. One day, the man found a pearl like no other he had ever seen! It was perfect! It was so beautiful that he was willing to sell everything he owned to have it!

No matter what we may have to give up in this life to follow Jesus, it will be worth it all!

Dear Father, may I be willing to give up all that this world has to offer to live with You one day in heaven. Amen.

Jesus and Me . . .

Jesus wants us to know that heaven is like the seeker's pearl. It is the **greatest** of all treasures. It should be sought after above all else. And heaven will be worth everything we own to have. Why? Because Jesus is there. And where Jesus is? That's where we want to be!

The Lost Sheep

Luke 15:4–7

Jesus once told a parable about a flock of sheep. One day, a little lamb wandered away from the flock and got lost. What did the **shepherd** do? Did he say, "I have plenty of sheep" and forget about it? No! He was a *good* shepherd. If even one of his little lambs got lost, the shepherd would search high and low until he found it. That's because he loved every one of them! It didn't matter how many sheep he had; he loved each one in a very special way. He searched and rejoiced to find the little lamb, and he brought it back to the fold!

Dear Father, You are my Good Shepherd. If ever I am lost and afraid, I will watch for You because I know You will come looking for me! Amen.

We have a **Good Shepherd** like that. His name is Jesus. He knows you and loves you very much. If you are ever lost and afraid, He will come looking for you, just like the shepherd in the parable looked for his little lamb. And Jesus will rejoice when He finds you and celebrate when you come home!

He Healed Many

· · · · · · · · · · · · · · · · · · ·

Matthew 8:1–3

Have you ever scraped your knee? It hurts! And it takes days to heal naturally. But when Jesus healed people, something supernatural happened. He healed them quickly and completely. The blind could see—immediately! Those who could not walk got up and walked—immediately! Natural healing can be slow, but the **supernatural** healing of Jesus was quick and complete.

One day, a man with a skin disease came and knelt before Jesus. He said, "Lord, you have the power to heal me if you want." He knew that Jesus was able to heal him, but he asked Jesus if He was willing.

Jesus touched the man and said, "I want to heal you. **Be healed!**" Immediately the man was healed!

The power to heal belongs to Jesus.

Dear Father, thank You for the miracle of healing. How You made me is amazing and wonderful! Amen.

All healing is a miracle from God. Just because it may happen slowly doesn't make it any less a **miracle**. God designed your body to repair itself when it gets hurt or infected by disease. Sometimes God may heal in an instant. That's a miracle! Sometimes it might take a little longer. But that's a miracle too. God restores us—sometimes fast and sometimes slow. But all healing is a wonderful miracle from Him!

He Forgave Sin

Mark 2:1–12

Jesus had the power to heal. He could make blind eyes see and deaf ears hear. But Jesus had the power to heal our souls as well as our bodies. We call sickness of the soul **sin**. And Jesus proved to a crowd that He had the cure for sin.

One day, some men carried their friend to see Jesus. The man was lame. They hoped Jesus would heal him. But when they got to the house where Jesus was, the crowd was too big. They could not get inside. So they climbed on the roof, cut a hole, and lowered their friend down on a mat. Jesus saw the man's crippled legs, but He knew this man needed more than healing for his body—he needed healing for his soul! Jesus said, **"Your sins are forgiven."**

The Pharisees were angry. They said to themselves, "Only God can forgive sins." But Jesus had authority on earth to forgive sins. So He commanded the lame man to stand up. The man stood and walked away with his mat!

Jesus has the power to forgive sin because He is the Son of God.

Dear Father, help me to forgive those who say and do things that hurt my feelings. May I forgive them as You have forgiven me. Amen.

Jesus had the **power** to forgive sins. But forgiveness isn't limited to Jesus alone. Sometimes *you* have to forgive. You can't forgive sins, but you can forgive those who sin against you! Jesus said that in the same way you forgive others, you will be forgiven. You have the power—the power to forgive others. To be like Jesus, learn to forgive!

He Fed Five Thousand

Mark 6:30–44; John 6:1–13

The news of Jesus' miracles began to travel far and wide. People came from everywhere to hear Him teach. One day, Jesus taught until late in the day. His disciples told Jesus to send the people away so they could get food. But to their surprise, Jesus said, "You give them food to eat."

The disciples didn't know how they were going to feed so many people. All they had was a boy's lunch of five loaves of bread and two fish. But Jesus took the food, blessed it, and began breaking it into pieces. More than **five thousand people** were fed that day with twelve baskets of food leftover.

Jesus fed everyone with a small boy's lunch!

Dear Father, I give You my time. I give You back the talent and treasure You have given me. I love You, Lord. Use my gifts in mighty ways. Amen.

Jesus and Me . . .

A little gift given to Jesus becomes a whole lot. That's because Jesus **multiplies** every gift a hundred times! Two fish fed over five thousand people! Five loaves of bread did the same. So when you give a little time, talent, or treasure to Jesus, get ready for a miracle! He will bless your gift and use it to help many people in so many ways!

He Ruled over Nature

Luke 8:22–25

Storms can be very frightening, can't they? Once, Jesus and His disciples were caught in a terrible storm. They were out on the lake in a boat. Waves crashed and the wind roared. And where was Jesus? He was in the back of the boat, fast asleep. The disciples woke Him, saying, "Master! Master! We will drown!" Jesus got up and **commanded** the wind and waves to be still. And in an instant, all was calm.

The One who created the winds and waves can most certainly control them!

Dear Father, You are only a prayer away. When I feel afraid and about to sink, I will call upon You. Thank You for always being there! Amen.

Jesus and Me . . .

Sometimes you feel like a disciple on a stormy sea. Something bad happens and you become afraid. You feel helpless and out of control. That's the time to call on the Lord. He will **answer** you. Sometimes He will calm the storm. Other times He will calm you and give you strength to go through the storm!

He Walked on Water

· ·

Mark 6:45–51

On another day, the disciples set out across the lake in a boat. It was getting dark when a powerful wind began to toss the boat up and down on the water. They rowed harder and harder, but it was no use. They could not get the boat to shore. Then they saw Jesus. He was walking toward them on the water! He said, "It is I! Do not be afraid." Then Jesus got into the boat, and the wind became calm. The One who made the waves can certainly walk on them.

Dear Father, help me to trust You more.
I know that no matter where I am or what
the situation, You will come to me! Amen.

Jesus and Me . . .

Jesus knows every circumstance and situation in your life. If you are happy, He knows it. If you are sad, He knows that too. Big decision? No problem. Jesus will **come to you** and will help you get through the difficult time—even if He has to walk on water! Nothing will keep Jesus away.

Peter Said Jesus Was the Christ

Mark 8:27–29

Who is Jesus? The people who saw Him do miracles asked this question. And people still ask it today. One day, Jesus asked His disciples, "Who do people say I am?"

They answered, "Some people say you are John the Baptist. Others say you are Elijah. And others say that you are one of the prophets."

But Jesus was much more than a man. He had come from heaven. So Jesus asked, "Who do you say I am?"

Peter answered, "You are **the Christ**." Peter believed that Jesus was more than a man. He was the promised Messiah, the Son of the living God, sent from heaven.

Peter understood who Jesus was and where Jesus had come from. We can too!

Dear Father, thank You for Jesus—King of kings, Lord of lords, the Deliverer sent from above to rescue and save me. Amen.

Jesus and Me . . .

The word **Messiah** is also used in the Old Testament.
The Hebrews were expecting Messiah to come.
He would be a King, a Priest, and a Prophet.
Jesus was all of these. The Messiah would also
be a Deliverer. Jesus was sent by God to be *our*
Deliverer. He delivered us from sin and death.
What a mighty God we serve!

Jesus Said He Is . . .

The bread that gives life. —John 6:35
The light of the world. —John 8:12
The good shepherd. —John 10:11–15
The way . . . the truth and the life. —John 14:6
The vine. —John 15:5

Jesus described Himself in many ways so people would know who He was. He said, "I am **the bread that gives life**" because in the same way bread fills an empty stomach, Jesus fills an empty heart. Jesus called Himself "**the light of the world**" because those who follow Him will never live in darkness.

He is **the Good Shepherd** because He takes care of us, and He is **the Way** because He guides us. He said, "I am **the vine**, and you are the branches," because when we stay connected to Jesus, He provides the strength we need.

Jesus has many names but only one purpose: He came to save us by being our bread, light, shepherd, vine, and way.

Jesus is everything we need.

Dear Father, everyone needs Jesus. Everyone needs His love and forgiveness. Help me be the one to share the message of grace with them. Amen.

Jesus *is* everything we need. But sometimes we confuse things we *need* with things we *want*. Jesus said that all things in this world are passing away. That would include gaming devices, TVs, and toys of every kind. They're not bad things; they're just things that will pass away. So He asks us to seek **eternal** things. Toys are fun and are things we want, but Jesus is something we need!

He Raised the Dead

Luke 8:41–56

Jairus was worried. His daughter was very sick. So he went to the One he knew could heal her. But before Jesus could get to Jairus's house, something terrible happened. Some men came to tell Jairus that his daughter had died. But Jesus paid no attention to what the men said. Instead, He spoke words that gave Jairus hope: "Don't be afraid. Just believe."

Taking Peter, James, and John with Him, Jesus continued on to the home of Jairus. Together they went into the room where the lifeless body of the little girl lay. Then Jesus took her hand and said, "My child, stand up!" Immediately she stood up!

Even the **power of life** and death belongs to Jesus.

Dear Father, You have given us minds to discover and invent such wonderful things. Yet I know that the power of life belongs to You alone! I praise You for who You are: the life-giving God! Amen.

Jesus and Me . . .

There are men and women who have done incredible things. They have built supersonic airplanes and skyscrapers. They have invented computers that guide spacecraft to far-reaching planets. But never forget this: only God can **create life**. The power of life and death are in His hands. He alone lives forever, and yet He offers that life to us in Jesus. In Him alone is life!

Why Does Jesus Have Authority on Earth?

Matthew 8:3; Mark 11:15–17; John 3:35; 5:27; 11:43–44

When an army officer shouts an order to his men, they obey! They do this because of a nine-letter word called *authority*. When you have authority, you have the power to tell others what to do.

Jesus had great **authority**. He had authority over sickness. When He said, "Be healed," the sickness had to leave. Jesus had authority over life and death. When He saw money changers buying and selling in the church, He stopped it. Why? Because Jesus had authority. "The Father loves the Son and has given him power over everything."

Jesus had power and authority given to Him by His Father.

Dear Father, I have no power without Jesus. He has given me authority over all the evil in this world when I pray in Jesus' name. Thank You for that power. Amen.

Jesus and Me . . .

The Bible says that God has not given us a spirit of fear. Instead, He has given us a **"spirit of power."** Jesus gave us that power and authority so we could walk in victory. He wants us to overcome evil with His authority! Because of Him, we have power over the enemies of God when we pray in Jesus' name!

Why Did Jesus Love Children?

Matthew 18:1–4; Matthew 6:25

Little children are very special to Jesus. He once told His followers, "You must change and become like little children. If you don't do this, you will never enter the kingdom of heaven."

So what did Jesus see in little children that He did not see in adults? **Little children have great faith**. They look to their parents to provide all that they need. Without worry, they depend on their mom and dad for food, clothes, and a place to live. Their faith in their parents is strong and never wavers.

Like children, everyone should depend on their heavenly Father for those very same things. "Don't worry," Jesus said. Depend on the Father for what you need. Children can do it. Can you?

Yes, there are some things that kids do much better than adults. And having faith is one of them. Jesus loves children and wants everyone to have their great faith.

Dear Father, I trust You. You are the one true God. By faith, I want You to be my God and walk with me always! Amen.

Jesus and Me . . .

Did you know that there is a big difference between **trust** and **faith**? Trust is *believing* that something is true. Faith is *acting* on your trust. Trust says, "That plane can fly." Faith gets on the plane. Trust says, "Jesus can save." Faith gives your heart to Jesus. Always let faith be your guide!

Where Did Jesus Bless the Children?

· · · · · · · · · · · · · · ·

Matthew 19:13–14

Jesus was born in Bethlehem in Judea. He grew up in Nazareth, a small village in Galilee. Just think of Judea and Galilee as states and Bethlehem and Nazareth as cities within those states. It was in Judea that Jesus blessed the children.

The people of Judea brought their children to Jesus. They wanted Jesus to pray for them. But His disciples thought Jesus was too busy, and they tried to send the children away. When Jesus saw this, He said, "Let the little children come to me. Don't stop them, because the kingdom of heaven belongs to people who are like these children."

And what are children like, you ask? They are people who trust in their heavenly Father.

Dear Father, one day I will be a grown-up. I know You see the person I will be someday. Guide and direct my life so that I will become the person You want me to be. Amen.

Jesus saw something in the **children** who came to Him—great potential! He saw a person who would one day build a church in the heart of Africa. He saw a doctor who would cure diseases and save the lives of many. What does Jesus see when He looks at you? I see a beautiful child who will one day do great things for the Lord!

Why Did Jesus Die on a Cross for Me?

Matthew 20:28

Jesus preached the most powerful sermons ever heard. But that was not enough to save us. He taught the crowds with parables, healed the sick, and cast out demons. But that was not enough to save us either. Jesus' greatest ministry was carried out on an old rugged cross. There, after living a perfect life, He died for you and me. And by His death and resurrection, Jesus gave that perfect life to you and me.

"The Son of Man came to give his life **to save** many people," Jesus said. He took our place in death. That was enough to save us!

He died to save us *from* God's wrath and to save us *to* heaven—all because He loves us.

Dear Father, I believe that Jesus died on a cross. I believe it was a necessary part of Your unfathomable love. Thank You. Amen.

It can't be explained. We believe it **by faith**. Of all the verses in the entire Bible, this one is the most challenging and can be accepted only by faith: without the shedding of blood, sin cannot be forgiven (Hebrews 9:22). The cross was necessary because God said it was necessary. Jesus died on the cross to save us *from* sin and *to* heaven. This we believe by faith.

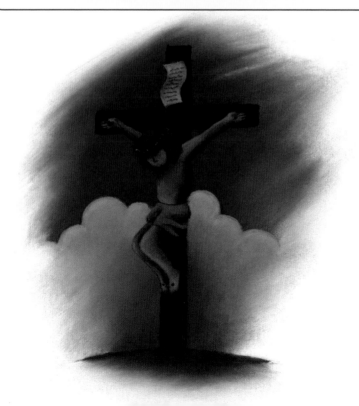

He Taught the Greatest Commandment

Matthew 22:36–39

· · · · · · · · · · · · · · · · · · · ·

Jesus was once asked which commandment was the greatest. He answered, "'**Love the Lord** your God with all your heart, soul and mind.' This is the first and most important command. And the second command is like the first: '**Love your neighbor** as you love yourself.'"

Jesus knew that **love** is the answer. People who love each other don't steal from each other. People who love each other don't lie to each other. If we love God, we will show our love by serving and obeying Him. And if we love each other, we will show our love by doing what is right.

Ask God to teach you to love!

Dear Father, I love You. Children of all ages have loved You too. That's because You are a wonderful God! Amen.

Jesus and Me...

Can you remember the very first Bible song you ever learned? Maybe it was "Jesus Loves Me." How about the very first Bible story or **Bible verse**? When Jesus was here on earth, children would learn a Bible verse found in Deuteronomy 6:5. It was called the *Shema*. It was the first and favorite of all Jewish verses. It says, "Love the Lord your God with all your heart, soul and strength."

He Taught That He Loves Us

John 13:34

We've all sung the words, "Jesus loves me, this I know." But do we know how much? To Jesus, *love* is an **action** word. He said, "You must love each other as I have loved you."

Jesus showed His love for us when He left His heavenly home and came to earth as a man. He suffered because He loved us. He was made fun of because He loved us. He preached the truth while people told lies about Him, all because He loved us. And eventually, He went to a cross to die. And why did Jesus do all of this? It's an easy four-letter word: **love**!

"Jesus loves me, this I know, for the Bible tells me so."

Dear Father, I want to be like Jesus. Teach me to love the way He did! Help me to put my love into action every day! Amen.

Jesus and Me . . .

Show the world that Jesus lives in your heart by your actions. Treat others with **kindness** and **respect**, just like Jesus. Sacrifice your time, treasures, and talents for others, just like Jesus. Show love to everyone, just like Jesus!

He Is Preparing a Home for Me

John 13:36–14:2

There were times when Jesus' disciples didn't understand some of the things He said. When Jesus said He was going away, they were troubled. "Where are you going?" Peter asked.

Jesus answered, "Don't let your hearts be troubled. Trust in God." Then Jesus began to speak about a place called heaven. "There are many rooms in my Father's house," He said. "I am going there to prepare a place for you."

And do you know what? Jesus is preparing a place in **heaven** for you too! Just think: your home in heaven may be next door to Peter's house!

Jesus is busy getting everything ready so that when we move out of this world, we can move right into His!

Dear Father, I should be busy. May I open my Bible each day and learn more about You. Help me to always do Your work! Amen.

We should be **busy** too! We should be busy reading our Bibles and learning about the things to come. We should be busy praying for those we love who may not know Jesus. We should be busy telling others that Jesus is coming back soon!

Jesus Said He Is Our Friend

John 15:12–15

Friends love to be together. They play together and spend time talking. They help each other at school. When bad days come, friends stick together. The Bible says that to *have* a friend, you must show yourself to *be* a friend. If we are going to show our friendship, we must do something for others.

Jesus said, "I call you **friends**." And to show Himself as a friend, He did an amazing thing. He said, "The greatest love a person can show is to die for his friends." Jesus not only called us His friends; He also showed us. He showed that He is our friend by dying on a cross to save us from our sins.

Wow! What a friend we have in Jesus!

Dear Father, I want to be a real friend to others. Help me live like You in front of them. Give me a special opportunity to tell them about You. Amen.

The **greatest thing** you can do for your friends is to live like Jesus in front of them! What does it mean to live like Jesus? Do the things He would do. Show the kindness He would show. Build others up by saying positive things. And when you have an opportunity, tell people why you are so happy. Tell them that knowing Jesus makes all the difference. That's what real friends do!

How Will We Know When Jesus Comes Again?

Matthew 24:31

T here are lots of instruments in an orchestra. The violin makes a sweet sound. Flutes sound the high notes, while tubas sound the low notes. But there is one instrument whose tone rises above all others—the trumpet. When the trumpet sounds, everyone can hear it. Trumpets are used to announce important events, victories, and the arrival of royalty.

Even to this day, kings and presidents are welcomed by the playing of a trumpet. So it is not surprising that the trumpet will announce the coming of the King of kings, Jesus Christ! The Bible says that a trumpet will sound, and every eye will see Jesus as He breaks through the clouds. Wow!

When the trumpet sounds, the whole world will hear!

Dear Father, I know that Jesus is coming again. But so many don't know He came the first time. They don't know why He came. Use me, Lord, to be a "trumpet." May I sound out the love and grace of Jesus! Amen.

Jesus and Me . . .

Jesus is coming again. And when He does, every person on the earth will see Him! But there are people **today** who do not know that He came the *first time*. So before God's trumpet sounds, sound your own trumpet! Use your voice to tell them about God's love. We don't want anyone to be surprised when Jesus comes!

Why Was Jesus Sent?

Luke 19:10

When something exciting happens in your life, something really great, what do you want to do? Do you clam up and zip your lips? Or do you rush to tell all your friends? Of course you want to tell everyone! And that's exactly what Jesus did. Jesus was sent from heaven with some really good news! And for three years, He preached that good news to anyone who would listen.

Jesus said He came **"to find lost people and save them**." To be "lost" means you have not heard about God's love. To be "saved" means you have heard and received God's love by inviting Jesus into your heart. It means you will live with Jesus forever in heaven. That's the good news—the best news! So now that you know why Jesus came, let's go tell everyone!

Jesus came to make God known to us.

Dear Father, thank You for Jesus. May I make Him known to all I meet. Amen.

Now that God is known to us, let's make Him known to **everyone**. Tell people that God created the heavens and the earth. Tell them that God has a wonderful plan for their lives. Tell them that Jesus loves them and is coming again to show them a love beyond measure! Jesus has made God's plan known. Now let's all make Jesus known!

Why Did the Pharisees Plan to Do Away with Jesus?

John 11:47–48; Luke 18:9–14

Pride is a small word that causes big problems. It was the reason the Pharisees sought to do away with Jesus. "This man is doing many miracles," they said. "If we let him continue doing these things, everyone will believe in him."

Jesus told His followers a parable that teaches the lesson of **pride**. He told about a Pharisee and a tax collector who went to the temple to pray. The Pharisee thanked God that he was better than other men. But the tax collector said, "God, have mercy on me. I am a sinner!"

When you feel that you are better than other people, that's called pride. The Pharisees let pride get the best of them.

Let's not let pride get the best of us!

Dear Father, may I be bold enough to tell others about You. May I be a lion, brave and strong in the Lord! Amen.

Jesus and Me . . .

Sometimes our pride keeps us from telling a friend about God's love. We don't want to risk being laughed at, so we remain as quiet as a church mouse. But the Lord isn't looking for a mouse. He's looking for a lion! He wants us to be **bold** in our witness. He says to us, "Be strong in the Lord. You can do it!"

Where Did Jesus Go to Pray?

· ·

Matthew 26:36–50

There was a small garden outside the walls of Jerusalem. It was called the **Garden of Gethsemane**. This was the place where Jesus went to pray the night He was arrested.

Peter, James, and John went with Jesus into the garden that night. Jesus asked them to watch and pray, but they fell asleep. Jesus prayed, "My Father, if it is not possible for this painful thing to be taken from me, and if I must do it, then I pray that what you want will be done."

Soon after this prayer, the soldiers came for Jesus. They followed Judas, who had led them to where Jesus was.

Dear Father, I know I can pray anywhere, anytime, any place. Thank You for listening to me! Amen.

Jesus and Me . . .

Where should we go to pray? It's true you can pray anywhere. Maybe you have a special chair or a favorite spot under a tree in your yard. Or maybe you like to go to your room to pray. Find a **quiet place** where you can be alone with God, and talk to Him right now!

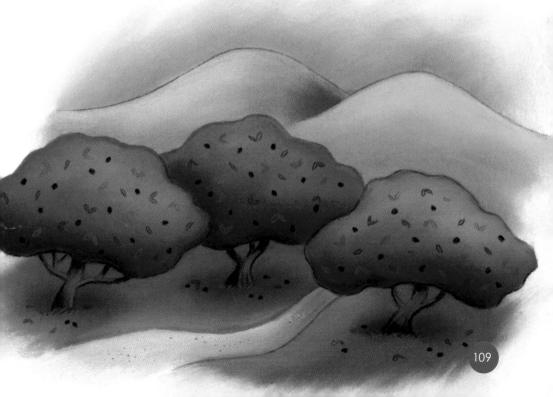

When Did Peter Deny Jesus?

Luke 22:31–62

Peter thought his faith was strong. He said, "Lord, I am ready to go to prison with you. I will even die for you." But Jesus said to him, "Before the rooster crows tonight, you will say you don't know me. You will say this three times!"

Peter couldn't believe it. That very night Jesus was arrested. It was so frightening. The disciples knew that prisoners were sometimes beaten and even killed.

So when a young girl recognized **Peter** as one of Jesus' followers, Peter said, "Girl, I don't know him." Three times Peter said he didn't know Jesus. The third time, while Peter was still speaking, a rooster crowed.

Then Peter remembered what Jesus had said, and he was filled with shame.

Dear Father, sometimes I am afraid. Sometimes I should tell others that I am a Christian, but I don't. Help me to never deny that You are my Savior. Amen.

Jesus and Me . . .

Sometimes fear can cause us to do things we wouldn't normally do. We might say something we wouldn't normally say. It happened to the great disciple Peter. It can happen to us too. If it does, remember that our God is **loving** and **forgiving**. Pick yourself up, and do better the next time. Peter did. You can too!

He Went to the Cross

Hebrews 9:22

Death is not something we like to think about much. But it is important to remember this: though salvation was freely given, it did not come without a great cost. And that cost is talked about in Hebrews 9:22: "And sins cannot be forgiven without blood."

It isn't a pleasant thing to think about, but our **salvation** cost Jesus His life. Jesus died on a cross for me and for you. He did it so our sins could be forgiven and so that one day we could live with Him in heaven forever! Jesus obeyed His Father and went to the cross, shedding His blood for you and me.

What a price Jesus paid for us!

Dear Father, may I stand up for Jesus. Make me ready to pay the price. Amen.

We might have to pay a price too. It's not popular to be a Christian. Some say that all religions lead to one God. Others will tell you that there are many ways to heaven. But Jesus said, "The **only way** to the Father is through me." That's because Jesus is the only one who gave His life so that our sins can be forgiven.

Where Did Jesus Die on a Cross?

Mark 15:22; John 19:17–30

The place where Jesus died has a name that sends shivers up my spine. It is Golgotha, which means the "Place of the Skull." It was a horrible place outside the walls of the city of Jerusalem. There, criminals who had done terrible things were punished. What in the world was Jesus doing in a place like that? He was showing His love for us.

On the hill called Golgotha, Jesus was crucified between two thieves. His mother, Mary, and His beloved disciple John listened as Jesus spoke His last words: "It is finished." After saying this, Jesus died.

Golgotha: it still sends shivers up my spine. Just think, the Son of God shed His blood for you and me.

Dear Father, thank You for sending Your Son to die for me. Thank You! Amen.

Jesus and Me . . .

Now all we have to do is believe! Jesus paid it all on the cross. He **paid the price** for your sin and my sin. He rose again to offer complete forgiveness to anyone who will receive Him as their Savior and Lord. He suffered so that we might be saved. He died so that we might live. What amazing grace He gives to all who believe!

When Was Jesus Raised from the Dead?

Luke 23:46; Matthew 12:40; Luke 24

Many heard Jesus speak His last words: "Father, I give you my life." After He said this, Jesus died. Some remembered Jesus saying, "Jonah was in the stomach of the big fish for three days and three nights. In the same way, the Son of Man will be in the grave three days and three nights." Jesus had said that He would rise from the dead. Would it actually happen?

On that Sunday, **three days after Jesus died**, Mary Magdalene and some other women found the tomb of Jesus empty. Where was He? An angel appeared to Mary Magdalene and told her He had risen! But did anyone see Him alive? Yes!

The Bible tells us that Jesus appeared to many people!

Dear Father, I know that Jesus lives because He lives in my heart. Amen.

Jesus and Me . . .

Jesus is still **appearing**. Not in bodily form but in Spirit. A hymn writer once wrote, "He walks with me, and He talks with me, and He tells me I am His own." Jesus is alive! And He appears in the hearts and lives of those who trust Him and have faith enough to walk with Him day by day!

He Rose from the Dead

Matthew 28:1–8

Jesus died on a Friday afternoon. Those who loved Him watched as His body was taken down from the cross. Many of His followers thought that all was lost and that maybe they had made a mistake. Maybe Jesus wasn't the Messiah. But they didn't know that Sunday morning was coming.

Mary Magdalene and another woman named Mary were the first to visit Jesus' tomb that Sunday. The large stone covering the entrance had been rolled away, and an angel spoke to them: "I know that you are looking for Jesus, the one who was killed on the cross. But he is not here. **He has risen**." The women ran to tell the disciples.

And that's what we must do. We must tell the world that Jesus has risen from the dead.

Dear Father, I rejoice to know that Jesus is alive and is living to wash away my sins! Amen.

Every religion in the world today had a beginning. All were founded by someone who is now dead— every religion but one! Praise God! We serve a **risen Savior**, who is in the world *today*. Christians rejoice because Jesus is alive! He is alive and sitting at the right hand of the Father in heaven. And we will see our risen Savior one day soon.

When Did Thomas Believe Jesus Was Risen?

John 20:24–29

The other disciples had already seen the risen Jesus, but Thomas had not. They told Thomas that Jesus was alive! But he said, "I will not believe it until I see the nail marks in his hands."

A week later, Jesus suddenly appeared to the disciples. He looked at Thomas and said, "Put your finger here. Look at my hands. Put your hand here in my side. Stop doubting and believe." Thomas was now sure it was true . . . Jesus was alive!

Jesus said to Thomas, "You believe because you see me. Those who believe without seeing me will be truly happy."

Dear Father, I see Jesus! I see Him with eyes of faith. Thank You for giving me that kind of faith. Amen.

Jesus and Me . . .

And we do believe without seeing. The Bible says that without faith it is impossible to please God. We believe by faith that Jesus Christ is the Son of the living God. We believe He is the **promised Messiah** who takes away the sin of the world. And we do all of this without seeing Jesus with our eyes. We live by believing, not by seeing (2 Corinthians 5:7).

He Taught Us to Go and Tell the Good News

Matthew 28:16–20

Come and see! We hear that a lot today. But Jesus taught His believers to do just the opposite. Just before He left to go back to heaven, Jesus told His disciples to go and tell! He said, "Go and make followers of all people in the world." This is the "great common mission," or the **Great Commission**, we have as Christians.

We must go and tell! The goal of every Christian is not to get people to come and see. Our goal is to get people into God's kingdom by going and telling them about God's love. We may go next door, or to another city, or even to another country. And Jesus promised that as we go, He will always be with us.

Jesus wants us to go and tell others about Him.

Dear Father, I want to go and tell (insert name) about Your love. Please open up a way for me to do that. Thank You. Amen.

Jesus and Me . . .

Think for a minute. Is there someone in your life who needs to know about Jesus? Maybe it's a friend. It could be your dad or mom, a sister or brother. Whoever it may be, think about that person right now. Jesus said that we should **go and tell** others about God's wonderful love. Let's pray for that opportunity right now.

He Taught That He Will Never Leave Us

Matthew 28:20; John 3:8

Jesus has made this promise to you: "You can be sure that I will be with you always." What a comforting promise! But sometimes we forget He's here because we can't see Him! I've learned a way that helps me know that **Jesus is always with me**. I think of the wind. You can't see the wind, but you know it's there when you see the leaves rustling in the breeze.

Jesus is like the wind. You can't see Him, but you can see all the wonderful things He has made, and you can see Him at work in the lives of His children. And one day you will see Jesus in person—coming in the clouds to take His children home for all eternity!

Dear Father, my eyes cannot see You, but I know You are real! Help me to feel your presence even when I can't see You. Amen.

The Bible says that we must **walk by faith** and not by sight. That's because our eyes cannot see all the things that exist. Eyes cannot see the wind, but windmill farms use the energy of the wind to create electricity. Our eyes cannot see God or His kingdom . . . yet. But one day we will! And it will be more real than the wind.

Where Is Jesus Now?

. . . .

Acts 1:1–11; John 14:2

After three days in the tomb, Jesus rose from the dead. He then spent forty days on earth encouraging His disciples and friends. He told His disciples that they were to tell the whole world what He had taught them. And after Jesus said this, His disciples watched as He rose up into the sky.

They were still looking up when two men in white robes appeared and said to them, "Why are you standing here looking into the sky? You saw Jesus taken away from you into heaven. He will come back in the same way you saw him go."

For Jesus had said, "There are many rooms in my Father's house. . . . I am going there to prepare a place for you."

Dear Father, I have a room in heaven because I am trusting Jesus to get me there! Amen.

Jesus and Me . . .

Have you made your reservation for a room in heaven? It's easy! If you believe that Jesus is your Savior and Lord and that He died on a cross to take away your sin, if you are ready to live your life for Him, your ticket to heaven is ready to go! And then . . . keep believing in your heart and telling others that Jesus is your Savior!

He Brought Salvation to the World

. . . .

Acts 4:12

What does the word *salvation* mean? It means you have been rescued. Rescued from what? Let's pretend you have become very sick. The doctor says only one medicine can save you. Would you take it? Of course you would!

Jesus is like a good medicine. We all have a condition called *sin*. Sin leads to death and separation from God. The Bible teaches us that "Jesus is the only One who can save people." No one else in the world is able to save us. That means **only Jesus can save us** from sin. He saves us like a good medicine.

When we invite Him into our hearts, Jesus becomes our salvation.

Dear Father, I know so many wait to hear the message of salvation. May I be the one to tell them! Amen.

Jesus and Me . . .

Millions of hearts are waiting. What are they waiting for? They are waiting for someone to tell them the good news of **God's wonderful love**. Who will go and tell them about Jesus? Maybe someday you will! Maybe God is preparing you to be the greatest missionary who ever preached a sermon! And maybe you will tell millions about Jesus!

The Region of Israel

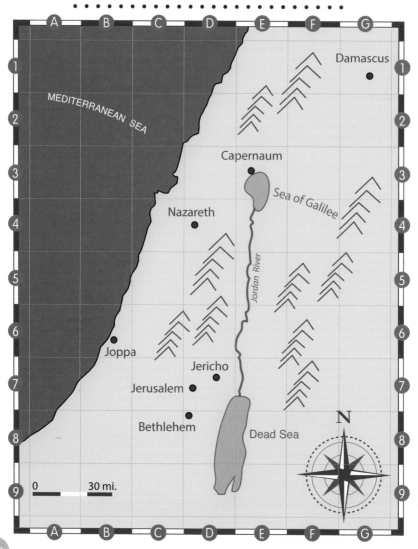

MEDITERRANEAN SEA

Damascus

Capernaum

Sea of Galilee

Nazareth

Jordan River

Joppa

Jericho

Jerusalem

Bethlehem

Dead Sea

N

0   30 mi.

Can You Find?

Nazareth	D•4
Jerusalem	D•7
The Sea of Galilee	E•3
The Jordan River	E•3—7
Bethlehem	D•8
Damascus	G•1
Capernaum	E•3
Joppa	B•6
Jericho	D•7
The Dead Sea	D•7—E•9

Where Did Jesus Grow Up?

Hint: page 24

Where Was Jesus Born?

Hint: page 16

By What Body of Water Did Jesus Call His Disciples?

Hint: page 40

Jerusalem (about AD 30)

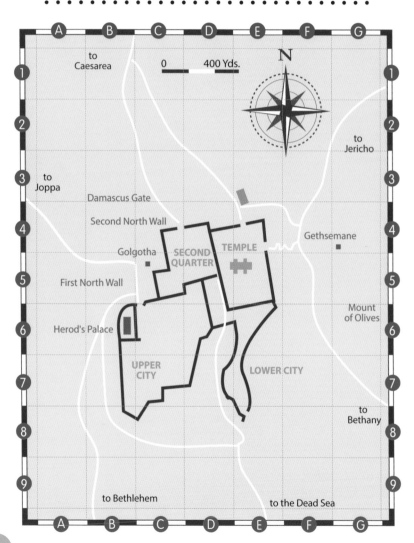

to
Caesarea

0   400 Yds.

N

to
Jericho

to
Joppa

Damascus Gate

Second North Wall

Gethsemane

Golgotha   SECOND   TEMPLE
QUARTER

First North Wall

Mount
of Olives

Herod's Palace

UPPER
CITY   LOWER CITY

to
Bethany

to Bethlehem   to the Dead Sea

Can You Find?

Where Did Jesus Go to Pray?
Hint: page 108

Do You Know Where Jesus Died on the Cross?
Hint: page 114

Can You Find Where Jesus Taught As a Boy?
Hint: page 22

133

When It Happened

In the beginning God created the sky and the earth.
—Genesis 1:1

600—500 BC

Zechariah the prophet said that Jesus' side would be pierced or stabbed: "They will look at me, the one they have stabbed. . . . They will be as sad as someone who has lost a firstborn son."
—Zechariah 12:10

AD 0—5

The angel Gabriel told Mary she would have a son, and He would be the Son of God: "You will give birth to a son, and you will name him Jesus. He will be great, and people will call him the Son of the Most High."
—Luke 1:31–32

The Baby Jesus was born! "While Joseph and Mary were in Bethlehem, the time came for her to have the baby. She gave birth to her first son."
—Luke 2:6–7

The angels visited the shepherds, and the shepherds went to see Baby Jesus in the manger: "So the shepherds went quickly and found Mary and Joseph."
—Luke 2:16

134

1500—1400 BC

Moses said this about Jesus:
"The Lord your God will give you a
prophet like me. He will be one of
your own people. Listen to him."

—Deuteronomy 18:15

800—700 BC

Micah said Jesus would be born in Bethlehem:
"But you, Bethlehem Ephrathah, are one of
the smallest towns in Judah. But from you
will come one who will rule Israel for me."

—Micah 5:2

800—700 BC

Isaiah said, "A child will be born to us.
God will give a son to us. . . . His name will
be Wonderful Counselor, Powerful God,
Father Who Lives Forever, Prince of Peace."

—Isaiah 9:6

AD 13—17

Jesus and His family went to Jerusalem for the Passover Feast: "When Jesus was 12 years old, they went to the feast as they always did."
—Luke 2:42

AD 30—35

Jesus was baptized by John the Baptist: "When all the people were being baptized by John, Jesus also was baptized."
—Luke 3:21

"When Jesus began to teach, he was about 30 years old."
—Luke 3:23

Today . . .

Jesus is preparing a home for us: "There are many rooms in my Father's house. I would not tell you this if it were not true. I am going there to prepare a place for you." Jesus promised to come back for us someday! "After I go and prepare a place for you, I will come back. Then I will take you to be with me so that you may be where I am."
—John 14:2–3

AD 30–35

"Jesus went everywhere in Galilee. He taught in the synagogues and preached the Good News about the kingdom of heaven. And he healed all the people's diseases and sicknesses."
—Matthew 4:23

AD 30–35

The Pharisees planned to kill Jesus:
"Then the leading priests and Pharisees called a meeting of the Jewish council. They asked, 'What should we do? This man is doing many miracles. If we let him continue doing these things, everyone will believe in him. Then the Romans will come and take away our Temple and our nation.' . . . That day they started planning to kill Jesus."
—John 11:47–48, 53

AD 30–35

Jesus was crucified on the cross: "Jesus cried out in a loud voice, 'Father, I give you my life.' After Jesus said this, he died."
—Luke 23:46

Jesus rose again! The angel said, "Jesus is not here. He has risen from death!"
—Luke 24:6

Jesus gave us the Great Commission: "So go and make followers of all people in the world. Baptize them in the name of the Father and the Son and the Holy Spirit."
—Matthew 28:19

"For God loved the world so much that
he gave his only Son. God gave his
Son so that whoever believes in him may
not be lost, but have eternal life."

—John 3:16